ELVIIRA KREBBER

Creator of the *Low-Carb, So Simple* blog

LOW SUGAR, SO SIMPLE

100 Delicious Low-Sugar, Low-Carb, Gluten-Free Recipes for Eating Clean and Living Healthy

FAIR WINDS

Brimming with creative inspiration, how-to projects, and useful information to enrich your everyday life, Quarto Knows is a favorite destination for those pursuing their interests and passions. Visit our site and dig deeper with our books into your area of interest: Quarto Creates, Quarto Cooks, Quarto Homes, Quarto Lives, Quarto Drives, Quarto Explores, Quarto Gifts, or Quarto Kids.

First Published in 2018 by Fair Winds Press, an imprint of The Quarto Group,
100 Cummings Center, Suite 265-D, Beverly, MA 01915, USA.
T (978) 282-9590 F (978) 283-2742 QuartoKnows.com

Fair Winds Press titles are also available at discount for retail, wholesale, promotional, and bulk purchase. For details, contact the Special Sales Manager by email at specialsales@quarto.com or by mail at The Quarto Group, Attn: Special Sales Manager, 401 Second Avenue North, Suite 310, Minneapolis, MN 55401, USA.

22 21 20 19 18   1 2 3 4 5

ISBN: 978-1-59233-779-8

Digital edition published in 2018

Library of Congress Cataloging-in-Publication Data

Krebber, Elviira, author.
Low sugar, so simple : 100 delicious low-sugar, low-carb, gluten-free
  recipes for eating clean and living healthy / Elviira Krebber.
ISBN 9781592337798 (pbk.)
1. Gluten-free diet--Recipes. 2. Sugar-free diet--Recipes. 3. Low-carbohydrate diet--Recipes.
RM237.86 .K74 2017
641.5/884--dc23
LCCN 2017027358

Design: Sarkar Design Studio
Page Layout: Megan Jones Design
Photography: Kristin Teig

Printed in China

The information in this book is for educational purposes only. It is not intended to replace the advice of a physician or medical practitioner. Please see your health-care provider before beginning any new health program.

I WOULD LIKE TO DEDICATE THIS BOOK
TO MY SON, LEO, WHO IS SIX YEARS OLD
AT THE TIME OF WRITING THIS BOOK.
ALWAYS REMEMBER
THAT HEALTHY FOOD IS THE SOURCE
OF ENERGY, LONGEVITY, AND, BELIEVE IT
OR NOT, IT IS THE BEST
MEDICINE AVAILABLE.

CONTENTS

INTRODUCTION

I used to be a real sugar addict. Thanks to my sweet tooth, I was overweight throughout childhood, and I was bullied at school because of it. (I was even heavier than the heaviest boys in the class!) My mom is an excellent cook, and whenever I was around, her pies, cakes, and cookies disappeared as quickly as she prepared them. When I knew she'd baked a delicious blueberry pie, I couldn't resist the temptation: I would cut one slice, then another, and another until there wasn't a crumb left! Inside, though, I was vulnerable and suffering from the constant bullying. I so desperately wanted to be thin that I started to cut calories drastically. Eventually I was diagnosed with anorexia.

After high school, though, I really lost control of my eating. I went back to eating sugar, and things got even worse. When I was studying industrial design close to the Arctic Circle, not a day would pass when I didn't indulge in a gigantic chocolate bar—and the endless darkness during the polar night exacerbated my sugar cravings. So it was no wonder that I started suffering from migraines and irritable bowel syndrome (IBS). I devoured pizzas and pastas, and poured copious amounts of sugar onto just about everything I ate. I bought cakes, muffins, candies—anything sweet—and ate them all at once. I knew it didn't do me any good, but I couldn't stop.

Later when I attended a language course in England, I enjoyed all the local "delicacies." My favorite was a super-supreme donut, a huge pastry filled with vanilla custard and coated with chocolate glaze. I gulped it down cheerfully along with a large chocolate milkshake. On the way home from school to my host family, I grabbed some humbugs—a local sweet—plus some fudge, and enjoyed them while walking. On my class trip to France, I bought a 14-ounce (400 g) bar of Toblerone and ate it in a single day. On the last day of the course, I celebrated by buying a huge carrot cake, which I divided with my roommate. (At least I didn't gobble it up all by myself, for a change!)

All that sugar made me feel miserable. Not only did I have physical ailments, but I was also suffering from depression, anxiety, and panic attacks. I had anorexia in my past, and now I developed another type of eating disorder: bulimia. I was frightened to death of vomiting, so I popped laxative pills like candies—dozens and dozens per day. Sitting in agony on the toilet didn't bother me much, as long as I got rid of the junk I'd eaten as quickly as possible.

Soon my condition worsened. I started suffering from unexplained stomach pains. In 1999, my colon was removed, and for a year after that I felt wonderful. However, the IBS symptoms came back, along with even worse pain. My weight plummeted until my BMI was only 12.7. I had arrhythmia, terrible stomach pains, and brain fog. No doctor could give me a diagnosis. The lab results all came back fine, but I felt like I was dying.

So I had no other choice but to take control of my health. I started to study nutrition, and soon I learned how destructive sugar is. I cut it out of my diet—and cereals, too, because I'd heard lots of success stories from people who regained their health by omitting gluten from their diets. (Little did I know at that point that cereals were, in practice, sugar. If that comes as a surprise to you, too, don't worry: I'll explain in the chapters that follow.)

As I quit sugar, I added more fat to my diet. It took a long time to understand how vital fat is to health—natural fat, that is. My brain fog finally disappeared after I started consuming butter and other natural fats.

NOTE TO THE READER

- All eggs used are U.S. size large, and should be organic and free-range whenever possible, because these contain more omega-3 fats and other nutrients. (Plus, they taste better!)

- Be sure to use the freshest ingredients and those of the best quality. Organic, non-GMO vegetables are best. As for meat and dairy products, choose those from animals fed with a species-specific diet. (For example, choose dairy and beef products that come from grass-fed cows.)

- Milk and cream should be organic, if possible, and free from food additives.

- All citrus fruits (especially lemons) should be organic and unwaxed.

- Baking powder should be aluminum-free. Cinnamon should be Ceylon cinnamon, or true cinnamon—not the more common cassia or Chinese cinnamon, which is toxic to the liver.

After I made these changes—quitting sugar and starch, and adding more fat to my diet—I started getting better. Much, much better. My weight normalized, and I was no longer bulimic; I suffered fewer migraines; and my anxiety and panic attacks disappeared. I wasn't depressed anymore. And my stomach finally felt great! No more IBS, no more bloating; all that crippling pain had disappeared. Now I enjoyed a flat tummy. I had six-pack abs without even trying. My entire body composition was ripped and muscular in comparison to the way it looked before. When I ate sugar—even when I wasn't overweight—I had a flabby stomach, enormous thighs, and a round face. Now my body looked toned and fit, even though I didn't do any sports.

With my new lifestyle, though, I noticed that it wasn't easy to find truly healthy recipes. In fact, most of the sugar-free recipes I came across didn't seem to be sugar-free at all. They contained dried fruit, syrups such as agave or rice syrup, or starches. Many of them had artificial sweeteners, too. I'd found healthy, sugar-free natural sweeteners myself, but couldn't find recipes for them. So I had to create everything from scratch. I developed recipes for breads, desserts, breakfasts, main courses, side dishes, and more—all with a minimal number of ingredients and steps, because I was busy and impatient.

Then in 2012, I established my *Low-Carb, So Simple* blog to help people in the same situation as I was—seeking easy, healthy recipes after switching to a low-sugar lifestyle. Five years later, I'm delighted to have more than 600,000 Facebook followers and hundreds of thousands of blog readers. There seems to be a huge demand for easy, truly healthy low-sugar recipes, and this is very understandable. With the current biased dietary guidelines and a food industry that spends billions on marketing its junk, people are getting sick, both literally and figuratively. They have to discover the truth behind these lies by themselves. Like parrots, doctors and dietitians still adhere to the low-fat religion, emphasizing the importance of "healthy" whole grains and fruit, not realizing that these substances actually make people sick.

Today we've finally started to understand that fat is your friend while sugar is the thing making you sick. Knowing that, we can move toward perfect health by savoring delicious, natural, clean food without sugar and starch. This book will show you how to do just that. Enjoy!

CHAPTER 1

THE SUGAR CRISIS

How Sugar Harms Your Body

Sugar is everywhere. Our diets are filled with it. Yet few people realize how harmful this extremely common ingredient is, and how damaging it is to our long-term health. Even though the World Health Organization (WHO) advises cutting sugar intake to a maximum of 25 grams a day, we often exceed this recommendation by more than three times: The average American consumes 76 grams of sugar per day.

Those of us who want to get off the sugar roller coaster find it nearly impossible. Sugar turns up everywhere: in our morning lattes; in our "healthy" breakfasts of yogurt and granola; in the cookies we snack on; and in our dinners of pasta with a side of bread. Sugar hides on our plates in plain sight.

Why Reducing Sugar Consumption Is More Important than Ever

Many modern diseases are caused or greatly exacerbated by too much sugar. We inundate our bodies with too much food-driven glucose, and consequently, our pancreases are exhausted and compromised from pumping out massive amounts of insulin to compensate for it. We also eat more frequently than ever before, which contributes to perpetually high blood sugar levels. It's a perfect storm that sets us up for a host of ills, from tooth decay to insulin resistance to metabolic syndrome and obesity. Even certain types of cancers and cardiovascular disease are linked to sugar overconsumption.

Obesity rates are the highest they have ever been—and they continue to increase. According to the National Health and Nutrition Examination Survey 2009–2010, two-thirds of the American population is considered overweight or obese. Today that figure is even higher. Nearly 30 percent of the world's population is obese, with the highest proportion residing in the United States, China, and India, according to the Institute for Health Metrics and Evaluation. The most distressing statistic is that obesity has increased in children and adolescent populations worldwide—more evidence that our sugar-laden diets are making us fat, sick, and tired, and are setting up the next generation for more of the same.

Our diets of sugar, starch, and refined-carbohydrate have created a veritable epidemic of type 2 diabetes because our bodies simply can't manage the burden of consistently high blood sugar levels. If current trends continue, the future doesn't look any brighter. The U.S. government estimates that 40 percent of Americans will develop diabetes at some point in their lives, while the International Diabetes Foundation projects that the worldwide incidence of diabetes is set to explode: It estimates that by 2040, more than 600 million people worldwide will have diabetes—a huge increase from the 2015 estimate of 415 million.

The price of our sugar-filled diets is expensive, and not just at the grocery checkout. Treating the diseases that stem from sugar overconsumption is very costly. Managing diabetes cost $245 billion in the year 2012 alone, according to the American Diabetes Association. This is a staggering statistic, considering that type 2 diabetes is solely caused—and is largely reversible—by lifestyle factors such as diet.

The Difference between Contemporary and Traditional Diets

At no time in history has the majority of the world's population been as inundated with access to food as we are today. Even as recently as one hundred years ago, consistently eating three meals a day was a luxury for much of the general population. Sugar was expensive, so it was enjoyed sparingly. Now the democratization of food, particularly sugar-laden foods, has made people fatter and sicker. This is true worldwide. Where people have given up their traditional diets in exchange for cheap, sugary, readily available processed food, health issues such as obesity, diabetes, cancer, and heart disease prevail. But how does our contemporary diet differ from the traditional diets of our grandparents, and why is our current pattern of eating so harmful?

One of the most striking differences between contemporary and traditional diets is—you guessed it—the amount of sugar we eat. During the past two centuries, our sugar consumption has skyrocketed. Americans consumed 129 pounds (59 kg) of added caloric sweeteners per capita in 2015, according to the U.S. Department of Agriculture's (USDA) Economic Research Service. Refined sugars consisted of 69 pounds (31 kg) of that amount. These added sweeteners, combined with high-carb intake from natural sources such as starch and fruits, increases the total amount of sugar consumed per person to sky-high levels. In comparison, according to the Kolp Institute, in the year 1770, the average American consumed only 4 pounds (1.8 kg) of sugar. See how much things have changed?

Not only do we regularly consume sweetened sodas and add sugar to our food, but the food industry also engineers common foods with sugar and sugar derivatives. Sugar lurks in everything, from condiments to soup to salad dressing. Fructose was once a rare type of sugar, occurring only in fruits and, in small amounts, certain vegetables. However, these days the food industry loves to add fructose to almost everything. Our food—sweet and savory alike—is saturated with different fructose-based syrups, particularly high-fructose corn syrup (HFCS).

As if this weren't bad enough, starch, which is also a form of sugar, makes up the majority of our diets. We start our mornings with sugary cereals, devour deep-dish pan pizza for lunch, and then consume plates of pasta with a side of crusty bread for dinner. Or we try to take the "healthier" route of fruit and oatmeal for breakfast, salad with a side of whole grain bread and a fresh-pressed juice for lunch, and some lean protein with a huge serving of brown rice for dinner. We congratulate ourselves for eating healthily, not realizing that such meals still contain massive amounts of sugar and sugar-like substances that our bodies can't handle.

The Role of the Food Industry in Promoting Sugar

Demonizing real food and promoting processed food as healthy and convenient has been the agenda of the food industry for several decades. It told us that butter and other natural fats humans have consumed for thousands of years were harmful, and would make us fat, and cause high cholesterol and cardiovascular disease. Naturally the food industry had a way to save us from these "unhealthy" saturated fats: low-fat, high-sugar products. But here's why those products aren't a solution: Humans evolved eating fat. When food lacks fat, we don't find it palatable. Fat gives food its appealing taste and texture, and it also triggers our body's natural satiety mechanisms, which let us know when we are full. Without it, the food industry had to heap on sugars, starches, and other additives to improve the taste and consistency of food. It was a cheap option that enabled the industry to mass-produce food with a long shelf life at a high profit.

Dietary guidelines have been around for almost a hundred years, but contrary to their original intent, our eating habits haven't improved, and we have not become healthier. In fact, we are sicker than ever. Although lifespans have increased, so has the incidence of chronic illnesses such as obesity, diabetes, cancer, and cardiovascular disease, which are directly correlated with poor diet and lifestyle choices. We may be living longer, but we are sick, fat, and miserable while doing it. Despite longer lifespans, the latest studies reveal bad news. Americans aren't just suffering from deteriorating health; their lifespans are also starting to decrease.

So what's wrong with the current dietary guidelines? Nearly everything, but let's start with the most obvious: sugar.

The newest attempt to control our eating, MyPlate, was launched by the USDA in 2015. It reflects little improvement on the former USDA food pyramid. Starchy foods such as beans and grains are no longer recommended as the base of our meals; now fruits and vegetables have taken their place. However, grains—that is, starches—are still a significant part of the MyPlate recommen-dations, as are sugary fruits; and starchy veg-etables are recommended in quantities that are far too high. Did you know that livestock are fed starch to fatten them up?

Despite the multiple studies and meta-analyses proving the efficacy of a low-sugar, reduced-carb diet, plus recent research debunking the idea that saturated fats cause obesity and heart disease, the dietary guidelines do not reflect these facts. They still try to fill our plates with sugar.

Though the recommendations state that healthy eating patterns should limit added sugar to a maximum of 10 percent of daily energy, they fail to clarify that our bodies don't differentiate between added sugars and naturally-occurring sugars in grains, fruits, and starchy vegetables—foods that MyPlate liberally endorses.

What Sugar Does to Your Body

By now you know that sugar is harmful—but how, exactly, does it affect your body? Let's take a look at why sugar is, quite literally, a toxic substance.

FIREWORKS IN YOUR BRAIN: Why Sugar Acts Like a Drug that Gets You High

We're going to start from the top—that is, with your brain. When you eat sugar, the abundant glucose almost literally creates fireworks in your brain. Yes, your brain needs glucose, but guess what? Your body can create all the glucose it needs by itself. This process is called *gluconeogenesis*, in which your liver transforms fats and proteins into sugar. Without this sophisticated system, humans wouldn't have been able to sur-vive famines. This means you don't need any carbohydrates (sugar) from your food, because your body can create all the sugar it needs. Seen in this light, it's even more difficult to understand, much less condone, the aggressive promotion of carbohydrates, starches, and other sugarlike substances by the current dietary guidelines.

I'm sure you've heard at least one of your friends confess, "I'm so addicted to sugar!" as she added sugar to her coffee or scarfed down a chocolate bar. Perhaps you've even said it yourself as you shared the last doughnut with your coworker. But can people actually become addicted to sugar, just like alcohol, nicotine, and other drugs?

Most of the scientists who have studied the effects of sugar on the body and brain would answer with a resounding "yes." There are several lines of compelling evidence that sugar is indeed as addictive and habit-forming as drugs. Here are two of them:

1. SUGAR LIGHTS UP BRAIN SCANS JUST LIKE DRUGS DO

In functional MRI scans, when people eat sugar, the reward centers of their brains "light up" in a pattern that's nearly identical to those found in people who take drugs such as cocaine or nicotine. Those images are very convincing that sugar affects the body in a similar way to drugs—and the potential to become addicted to sugar is there from the first bite.

Much of this type of research has been directly led or inspired by David S. Ludwig, M.D., Ph.D., at Harvard Medical School. In one of his research papers, he provides evidence that simple sugars such as sucrose (table sugar) and fructose, with a very high glycemic index, cause the reward centers in the brain to immediately light up. However, he also provides evidence that high-fiber complex carbohydrates, with a low to medium glycemic index, do not have this profound effect.

2. CUTTING SUGAR COLD TURKEY CAN LEAD TO SYMPTOMS OF WITHDRAWAL

Sugar addicts who cut their sugar intake cold turkey undergo withdrawal symptoms similar to those that accompany withdrawal from powerful drugs such as nicotine, amphetamines, and cocaine. These symptoms include intense cravings, the desire to binge, severe headaches, body aches and pains, dramatic mood swings, and the "shakes." These are the classic signs of addiction withdrawal.

If you are addicted to sugar, you will never conquer that addiction simply by cutting back on added sugar. Just think about it: Can cocaine addicts kick their cocaine addiction by cutting back on cocaine? Of course not!

To conquer your sugar addiction, you'll need to cut out sugar completely. This includes not only processed foods, but also *all* sugars, including starchy foods such as pasta and bread. So be sure to read food labels carefully. Better yet, try to make all your food from scratch so you'll know for sure that you're avoiding all sugar. Don't eat out or buy food from delis. Don't worry, you won't go hungry. In the recipe section of this book, you'll find many easy, mouthwatering recipes to help you get started with sugar-free pantry staples, breakfasts, lunches, dinners, snacks, desserts, and drinks.

UNHAPPY HEART: Cardiovascular Diseases Are Caused by Excess Sugar Consumption

Before you pour that sweetened creamer into your coffee, you may want to put your hand on your chest and pledge to be kinder to your heart. Overindulging in sugar is one of the worst things you can do for your cardiovascular system. Numerous scientific studies show that eating too much sugar directly damages your heart tissue and can lead to atherosclerosis (hardening of the arteries).

The inflammation sugar causes in your body damages your veins and arteries. Here's how: The fat that's accumulated in your body after eating too much sugar and starch releases inflammatory compounds into your blood, and these compounds injure the blood vessels. Sugar-consumption-induced inflammation is what promotes plaque and heart disease—not the cholesterol or the fat you eat.

If this information isn't enough to put you off sugar, consider the advice given by the American Heart Association, which has been promoting the results of a large-scale 2014 study that clearly demonstrated that eating too much sugar can significantly reduce your lifespan—and your quality of life. The study found that individuals who consumed 17 to 21 percent of their average daily calories from added sugar had a 38 percent higher chance of dying from a cardiovascular disease, such as a heart attack, than those who consumed only 8 percent of their average daily calories from added sugar. The study refers only to *added* sugar, not the overall sugar content of the food. The study went on to assert that individuals who received more than 21 percent of their average daily calories from added sugar were twice as likely to die from a heart attack or another cardiovascular disease.

Sobering, isn't it? And it may come as a bit of a surprise. Although most people seem to know that sugar can make you gain weight, cause diabetes, and rot your teeth, not as many people know that sugar can clog your blood vessels and bring on a heart attack.

TORTURE TO YOUR TUMMY:
How Sugar Damages Your Gut

Sugar also causes havoc with your gut flora—that is, the microorganisms that live symbiotically in your gut. You've probably heard about good bacteria and bad bacteria, right? In a human with a healthy gut, her good bacteria will far outweigh her bad bacteria, and she'll also have a healthy balance of bacteria species. And Candida—a harmful type of yeast—will only be present at low levels. Eating too much sugar upsets the balance of your gut flora. Your gut becomes rife with bad bacteria, such as the *Enterococcus* species (which causes diverticulitis, urinary tract infections, endocarditis, and meningitis); *Clostridium innocuum*, *Catenibacterium mitsuokai*, and *Eubacterium dolichum* (all of which, in large amounts, are pathogenic and highly resistant to antibiotics); and *Clostridium difficile* and *Clostridium perfringens* (which cause foodborne illnesses).

What's more, too much sugar causes a rise in Candida species, especially in women. Candida can cause vaginal yeast in women. If they recur, it's likely that Candida is also invading other tissues in your body, which is why you may feel exceptionally tired and achy if you have a vaginal yeast infection. Even worse, Candida is strongly linked to leaky gut syndrome, in which the lining of your gut becomes so porous that it leaks out its contents into your bloodstream. This in turn is associated with blood poisoning, chronic fatigue syndrome, food intolerance, painful joints, and autoimmune diseases. When you combine sugar-related leaky gut with the consumption of grains, it's no wonder there are so many people in the world suffering from serious diseases nowadays.

WATCH YOUR WAIST: It's Mainly Sugar that Makes Us Overweight

Sugar is notorious for causing belly fat. But what exactly does *belly fat* mean?" Well, when the circumference of your waist expands, it can be caused by two different layers of fat:

1. The subcutaneous layer of fat embedded just below the inner layer of belly skin. This is the fat that you can actually pinch, along with your loose belly skin.

2. The visceral fat that surrounds all the visceral organs, such as the liver, pancreas, stomach, and intestine. This layer of fat is hidden within the abdominal cavity, so you can't pinch it.

When Santa Claus chuckles "Ho Ho Ho!" and his belly jiggles and wiggles like a bowl full of jelly, that's subcutaneous fat. Visceral fat doesn't jiggle. In fact, you can have a rock-hard belly that's loaded with thick layers of visceral fat.

Both types of belly fat affect our waist circumference, but the lumpy fat you can see in the mirror is the subcutaneous fat. When you see your belly start to protrude but you can't pinch it, this may be an indication that your visceral fat is growing.

Although it may not look as "ugly," visceral fat is far more dangerous than subcutaneous belly fat because it interferes with the function of your organs. It can prevent your liver from producing bile, thereby interfering with fat breakdown and waste elimination. It can prevent your pancreas from sending out hormones such as insulin when they're needed most—that is, to handle the truckload of carbs you just ate. It can raise your cholesterol and blood pressure and increase your risk for breast and colon cancer.

INSULIN SENSITIVE, PREDIABETIC, DIABETIC: Why Constant Sugar Consumption Leads to Diabetes and Metabolic Syndrome

Excessive sugar consumption is one of the primary causes of type 2 diabetes. This is the noncongenital kind of diabetes that develops over time, usually due to a combination of lifestyle issues (overeating, eating too much sugar, and being overweight) and genetic predisposition.

If type 2 diabetes runs in your family, you need to be especially concerned about keeping your sugar intake low. Your carb tolerance probably isn't very good, and will worsen over time. But the good news is that type 2 diabetes can be treated and prevented by diet alone. That means avoiding sugar and finding your ideal personal level of daily carbs. (Don't be surprised if that turns out to be as low as 30 grams or fewer of net carbs daily.) The only way to discover your ideal daily carb level is to experiment. When your weight stabilizes and you have no negative symptoms, you'll know you've gotten it right.

To help you understand why sugar consumption can lead to diabetes, or causes it to appear earlier than it should if you are genetically predisposed to it, I'm going to give you a little biology lesson. Right behind your stomach (toward your back) is the pancreas, an organ about the size of your hand. Part of the pancreas's job is to crank out digestive enzymes. It usually does this very well, even in type 1 diabetics.

The smallest part of the pancreas has the most powerful role to play. This area is called the *islets of Langerhans* and it consists of clusters of highly specialized cells that produce powerful hormones that control your food metabolism. (The unusual name comes from the German scientist who discovered them.) The most famous of these are the beta cells, which produce insulin. In a healthy nondiabetic person, beta cells respond to glucose in the bloodstream by producing just the right amount of insulin needed to help the glucose cross over the membranes of all the various cells in the body and to act as fuel for the cell and all its functions, such as DNA repair and sending chemical messages to other cells.

When you eat too much sugar, your beta cells are forced to work overtime to produce extra insulin. This isn't usually a problem in your childhood, teens, or twenties, because you probably have a young, vibrant body with young, vibrant beta cells. However, with each passing year, it becomes increasingly difficult for your beta cells to keep up with the high demand for insulin if you continue to overeat sugar. If you have inherited genes that make you more susceptible to developing type 2 diabetes, your beta cells deplete even faster.

A study published in *Diabetes Care* revealed that type 2 diabetes is associated with a 60 percent increased risk for dementia, while earlier studies also indicate that even slightly elevated blood sugar levels boost the risk. In fact, Alzheimer's disease is often called *type 3 diabetes* because Alzheimer's disease involves a similar problem with insulin resistance, but in its case, the damage mostly affects the brain instead of the body. (Yet another way in which sugar harms the brain.) Here's what this means for you.

- If you have family members with type 2 diabetes, then you need to be especially protective of your beta cells and other specialized cells in the islets of Langerhans. That means you need to lay off the sugar. Pull out all the stops and break your sugar addiction right now! Your life may literally depend on it. You'll also want to avoid overeating in general, because this can also overwork the cells in the islets of Langerhans.

- If you don't have a family history of diabetes, you still should be careful. Overeating sugar can still wear out your beta cells and cause you to develop type 2 diabetes over time.

LETHALLY LANGUISHED LIVER: Why Fructose Consumption Is a Main Cause of Fatty Liver Disease

Fatty liver disease occurs when more than 5 to 10 percent of the liver consists of fat. The type of fatty liver disease caused by sugar overconsumption is sometimes called non-alcoholic fatty liver disease (NAFLD) to distinguish it from fatty liver disease caused by consuming too much alcohol. Sugar can be just as destructive to your liver as alcohol, and the damage it does is essentially the same. Like type 2 diabetes, it's become something of an epidemic. According to a review published in the *Journal of American Medicine (JAMA)*, NAFLD affects about 75 million to 100 million individuals in the United States alone. That's not a typo. (In various parts of the world, 9 to 37 percent of people have NAFLD.) Worse, the potential morbidity of NAFLD extends way beyond the liver: fatty liver disease, cardiovascular diseases, and metabolic diseases go hand in hand.

This is bad news because your liver is essential to your survival. It is one of the primary organs responsible for detoxifying our systems—and with all the pesticides, herbicides, PCBs, heavy metals, solvents, and food additives to which our bodies are exposed each day, our livers deserve a little more respect. Plus, the liver is responsible for fat metabolism. It produces the bile that allows the intestines to break down fat and utilize it as energy; it removes and processes fat from the bloodstream; and it recycles old blood cells. These are just a few of the reasons to love your liver and to protect it from fatty liver disease.

One of the best ways to do that is to cut the sugar. In the next chapter, you'll find out where sugar hides and how to spot it in its many guises.

CHAPTER 2

STEALTH SUGAR

Sugar in Its Many Forms

Sugar is sugar, right? Yes, but it's not quite that simple.
This chapter will show you how—and why—sugar turns up as
sweeteners and in foods under a wide range of names, and will
explain why you should avoid all of them, including starches.
Let's begin by talking about sugar in its simplest form.

Monosaccharides: Simple Sugars

All sugars and all carbohydrates are built with basic building blocks called *simple sugars*. From chocolate chips to potatoes, you essentially need three atoms (carbon, hydrogen, and oxygen) to create the building blocks for all sugars and carbs. Simple sugars are the most basic building blocks for all other sugars. That is, chemically speaking, they cannot be broken down any further. Thus they're called monosaccharides (*mono* means "one" or "single," and *saccharide* means "sugar"): literally, *single sugars* made of only *one* of the simplest building blocks of all known sugars and carbohydrates.

There are dozens of naturally occurring simple sugars that can serve as building blocks for complex sugars and carbohydrates, but there are only three simple sugars that that are used to build virtually all of the sugars and other sweet ingredients we cook and bake with. They are glucose, fructose, and galactose. Whether you add brown sugar, apple juice, honey, dates, or agave syrup to your recipes, the sugar in them will be broken down into those three simple building blocks. (Sugar is sugar!) Your body processes each of the three simple sugars differently. Here's how.

Glucose

Glucose, also called dextrose, corn sugar, grape sugar, and blood sugar, was the first simple sugar to be isolated and identified. The name *glucose* comes from the Greek word for sugar—*glyk* or *gluc*—and the Latin word *ose*, meaning "full of." Thus glucose literally means "full of sugar." Following the same pattern, as other sugars have been identified, they've been named with the *-ose* suffix, too.

Glucose is absorbed into the bloodstream by the small intestine. Once it enters the bloodstream, insulin helps it penetrate the cell membrane, where it's used to fuel every biological process in the body, from your brain cells to the muscle cells in your feet.

However, glucose is not the only source of energy available to our cells. They also function well on ketone bodies if glucose is not available due to fasting, or restricted consumption of carbohydrates and protein. (True, some cells still need glucose to work, but remember that our livers can process all the glucose necessary to cell function.) Much work is being done on the benefits of following a ketogenic diet, which prohibits sugar and restricts proteins, and may particularly help people suffering from obesity, diabetes, neurological disorders, and even cancer.

Fructose

Fructose—or levulose—is another common simple sugar, and gives fruit and fruit juices their sweet flavor (hence the name). Fructose also accounts for a significant portion of honey, agave, and even molasses processed from sugar cane. It is sweeter than glucose: If the sweetness of glucose is 0.8 (table sugar being 1.0), fructose's sweetness perception rating is 1.75.

Fructose cannot be absorbed by cells and used directly for energy like glucose and ketone bodies. Instead fructose is transported directly to the liver for processing (without the aid of insulin). After conversion to glucose, it's either used for energy or stored as glycogen or fat—which means it's one of the main culprits in obesity and fatty liver disease.

Galactose

Galac means "milk," so the word *galactose* literally means "milk sugar." But wait a minute: Everyone knows that the sugar in milk is lactose, right? Yes, but lactose molecules are actually composed of two simple sugars: glucose and galactose.

In nature, lactose and galactose occur rarely outside mammalian milk. That means lactose can't be utilized directly by the body. In fact, it will rot in the intestine if it isn't broken down into glucose and galactose. Once this happens, the glucose is easily utilized by the body, but not the galactose: most of it has to be converted to glucose before it can be processed.

Glucose or Fructose: Which Is Worse?

There's a raging debate around which is worse for you: glucose or fructose; and table sugar (which is half glucose and half fructose) or plain fructose. Articles and blog posts with this basic message abound:

- Glucose (and table sugar) is digested faster than fructose and causes a big spike in your blood glucose level.

- Fructose is processed more slowly (by the liver), so it doesn't cause a sudden rise in your blood glucose level.

- Glucose, therefore, is worse for you than fructose. It causes you to gain more weight and it leads to diabetes and metabolic diseases more often than fructose.

Unfortunately, much of this argument originated with carefully crafted (and well disguised) marketing campaigns by the food associations that wanted to sell you on the idea that high fructose corn syrup (HFCS) is good for you—or at least no worse than ordinary table sugar.

Here's the truth in a nutshell. Multiple scientific studies have proven that excess fructose has a much greater negative effect on your body and health than excess sucrose, although neither is good for you. Excess fructose seems to be more likely to create belly fat, specifically visceral fat—especially around your heart and in your arteries. Last but not least, fructose seems to stimulate the onset of diabetes and other metabolic diseases more than table sugar.

Disaccharides

Many of the sugars added to food are made by joining two simple sugars together. These are called disaccharides, where *di* means "two" and *saccharides* means "sugars." Here are three common ones:

1. **Sucrose (sugar, table sugar, saccharose, white sugar, crystalline sugar, cane sugar, or beet sugar).** This is probably the most commonly used sweetener. It's made up of one molecule of glucose loosely linked to one molecule of fructose, and it's easily broken into glucose and fructose by our bodies.

2. **Maltose (malt sugar, maltobiose, monosaccharide glucose, and disaccharide maltose).** Maltose is made of two molecules of glucose loosely linked together. It's often found in malt, beer, cereal, pasta, potatoes, and many processed food products.

3. **Lactose (milk sugar).** As discussed previously, the lactose molecule is composed of one glucose molecule and one galactose molecule that can only be broken apart by a special enzyme, lactase.

Different Forms of Sugar Cane Sucrose

Sucrose made from sugar cane isn't a single item. It comes in many guises, and here are a few of the main ones.

NAME	ALSO KNOWN AS	PROCESSING	COLOR/ APPEARANCE	SUITABLE FOR A LOW-SUGAR LIFESTYLE?
Refined sugar	White sugar, pure sugar, table sugar	Phosphatation uses phosphoric acid to remove what the sugar industry calls "impurities"—the natural molasses containing vitamins and minerals. Then it's bleached with sulfur oxide, which leaves trace amounts of sulfur in the sugar, before carbonation and liming. It's still somewhat brown in color, so it's run through bone char, or burnt bone, to "deodorize" it. Finally, it's subjected to isopropyl alcohol to wash away residual molasses. (Yummy? Not really.)	White, fine-grained	No
Organic sugar		Like other organic products, certified organic sugar is never sprayed with pesticides or herbicides. However (unlike other organic products), the way in which organic sugar is processed is entirely different to the method described above. So, it will have no residual chemicals, and it will retain some of the molasses, yielding a richer taste and slightly darker color.	Light brown	No
Sucanat	Rapadura, panela, muscovado, *khaand*, jaggery	Sucanat is a both brand name and contraction for the French term *sucre de canne naturel*, which translates literally to "sugar of the natural cane," or sugar from sugar cane. It contains much of the molasses.	Medium-dark brown; coarse crystals	No

NAME	ALSO KNOWN AS	PROCESSING	COLOR/ APPEARANCE	SUITABLE FOR A LOW-SUGAR LIFESTYLE?
Raw sugar		This is unbleached and less processed than pure white sugar, but the amount of processing it's subjected to varies. Many raw sugar products may have been chemically treated, so may contain chemical traces. The sugar cane may have been sprayed with pesticides and/ or herbicides. Raw sugar is usually made from sugar cane, not beets, because molasses from beets has an unpleasant taste—but there are no laws preventing companies from producing raw sugar from beets.	Light brown	No
Turbinado sugar	Sugar in the raw	Turbinado sugar is less processed than pure white sugar. It is usually made from the first press of the sugar cane, which contains less molasses than the second and third presses. The molasses it does contain usually isn't chemically removed. It's much more natural than light brown sugar. Organic turbinado sugar is essentially organic sugar with less of the molasses removed.	Light brown	No
Brown sugar	Light brown sugar; dark brown sugar	Brown sugar may look more natural than white, but it's not. It's highly processed white sugar to which molasses has been added before being dried again. Dark brown sugar has more molasses mixed back in than light brown sugar.	Light or dark brown; medium to fine crystals	No
Evaporated cane juice		This is processed raw sugar water with an undetermined amount of molasses, or inverted sugar syrup (see next page). The U.S. Food and Drug Administration (FDA) does not require any standard for ingredients labeled as evaporated cane juice.	Clear	No

Syrups and Saps

Sugar doesn't have to be in solid form. Here are some common sweeteners that are syrups or saps.

NAME	ALSO KNOWN AS	PROCESSING	SUITABLE FOR A LOW-SUGAR LIFESTYLE?
Honey		Produced naturally by bees, honey is one-third fructose. It contains an array of healthy ingredients, such as proteins, amino acids, organic acids, vitamins, and minerals.	No
Molasses	Black treacle	The byproduct of refined pure white sugar production, molasses contains vitamins, minerals, antioxidants, and micronutrients—but it's processed by the body in the same way as granulated white sugar. Different varieties depend on how concentrated it is and the sugar cane press from which it's derived. Pure blackstrap molasses, taken from the third press of the sugar cane, is considered to have the highest flavor quality and the most vitamins and minerals.	No
Agave syrup		Extracted from the blue agave plant, agave syrup has a high fructose content—between 50 and 90 percent. Some health experts consider it more harmful than even HFCS, which is about 55 percent fructose. It's highly refined and may contain harmful residual chemicals, such as sulfuric acid and dicalite.	No
Corn syrup		Made by breaking down cornstarch, regular corn syrup (as opposed to HFCS) consists almost entirely of glucose. The process by which it's made is somewhat industrial, but it's nowhere near as industrial as converting corn syrup into HFCS. Unless its label clearly states that it's non-GMO (or is organic), most corn syrup is made from GMO corn.	No
Maple syrup		The concentrated sap of maple trees, a product labeled as "maple syrup" must be at least 66 percent sugar, according to North American law. Its sugar is almost entirely sucrose, so your body treats it just like table sugar, even though it contains a high concentration of vitamins and minerals, which give it a unique, rich taste.	No
Inverted sugar syrup		This is sugar water (from highly processed refined sugar) in which the glucose and fructose have been separated from the disaccharide sucrose molecule and left suspended in fluid. It has a sweeter taste and makes baked goods stay moist and fresh for longer.	No

NAME	ALSO KNOWN AS	PROCESSING	SUITABLE FOR A LOW-SUGAR LIFESTYLE?
Sweet sorghum	Sorghum molasses	This is made from several closely related sorghum grass species that originated in Africa (and were brought to the United States by African slaves). Labor-intensive processing has led to a drop in production recently, but it's still prized by many Southern cooks. Although it tastes like molasses, it has a distinctive flavor—and slightly fewer vitamins and minerals. About 85 percent of the sugar in sweet sorghum is sucrose. The remaining sugars are fructose and glucose.	No

Starch and Other Complex Carbs

Now you've gotten a crash course in simple carbs. But what about complex carbs? As you know, all carbs are sugars, and sugars are also known as saccharides. This includes complex carbs, such as the starch in potatoes, rice, beans, corn, oats, wheat, and many other plant-based foods. In our everyday language, *sugar* refers only to sweet-tasting carbohydrates. However, chemically speaking, complex carbs are just sugars with a more complicated structure. Their most basic building blocks are simple sugars, usually sugar rings. This means that complex carbs, such as starches, are compound sugars. That's why they're called *polysaccharides*, which literally translates as "many sugars."

Starch

Starch is the form in which plants store extra glucose they don't immediately use. When we eat a potato or a piece of bread full of plant starch, our bodies break down that starch into the basic building blocks of glucose, which we can then use for immediate energy or convert into another form of glucose storage—glycogen. (Or, if our carb intake exceeds our individual tolerance, that glucose can be converted into body fat.)

Glycogen

Plants store glucose in the form of starch, and animals, including humans, store glucose in the form of glycogen, which, like starch, is made from thousands of glucose molecules bonded together. We store glycogen primarily in our liver and muscle cells, but we can also store a little glycogen in our kidneys and the glial cells in our brains. (Glial cells are the most abundant cell type in the brain, comprising nearly 90 percent of the brain.) We also consume a small amount of glycogen when we eat meat because it is stored in the muscle tissues of other animals.

Cellulose

Some polysaccharides are used to form rigid structures. Cellulose, also formed by bonding together thousands of glucose molecules, is used to form the cell walls of plants and algae. It's what makes redwood trees stand up tall and cotton and hemp such sturdy fibers for clothing. Humans don't have the enzyme

WHAT IS HIGH-FRUCTOSE CORN SYRUP?

A combination of fructose and glucose, high-fructose corn syrup (HFCS) appears on food labels under several names, including HFCS, isoglucose, glucose-fructose, and glucose-fructose syrup. Here's why it's high fructose: Much of the glucose in corn syrup has been converted to fructose to make it sweeter and more stable (after all, a longer shelf life means more profit for food manufacturers).

It gets worse. When the portion of fructose in the syrup is increased even further through industrial chemical processes, it's renamed, and may appear on labels as HFCS-90: a corn syrup that is 90 percent fructose. (As if the regular stuff weren't bad enough.) Whatever you call it, it's super-sweet and very harmful. Made from GMO corn, many scientific studies have linked the introduction of this industrial "sugar" into our food supply to a sharp, dramatic rise in obesity, type 2 diabetes, heart disease, and many other metabolic diseases. You should avoid HFCS completely.

Get into the habit of reading the ingredient label of every product you buy. This is where you will find the hidden sugars—even if the product itself isn't sweet. Look for, and avoid, any word that ends in -ose. As discussed earlier, this indicates the presence of sugar as well as syrups, including oat syrup, rice syrup, agave syrup, molasses syrup, invert syrup, and, of course, HFCS. Steer clear of diastatic malt, cane juice, blackstrap molasses, and barley malt. These are all forms of sugar, too.

necessary to digest cellulose, so we excrete it. From cellulose, we get those insoluble fibers that are vital for healthy digestion.

Starch Digestion

Starch is composed of two types of glucose chains: amylose and amylopectin. As you chew your starch-rich food, the saliva in your mouth mixes with your food and starts to digest it before you even swallow. After you swallow, the enzyme amylase continues to break down the starch until it enters the stomach, where stomach acid stops it. But once the partially broken-down starch enters your small intestine, the pancreas sends in more amylase, until it's broken down into maltose, a sugar composed of two glucose molecules bonded together. Then another enzyme, maltase, breaks those glucose molecules apart, and eventually shorter intermediates are formed, most of which are

called maltodextrin. The sweet receptors in your brain can detect maltose, but it is nowhere near as sweet as sucrose, fructose, or glucose. This means you're consuming sugar without being aware of it.

The food industry sneaks maltodextrin into all sorts of processed foods—especially junk foods such as potato chips, soft drinks, candy, and granola bars—so it's no wonder we get so addicted to these foods without knowing why. It looks like we may not be just addicted to simple sugars, but also to the added maltodextrin, which may light up the pleasure portion of the brain in the same way that sugar does.

All this means that reducing the amount of starch we consume is one of the keys to quitting sugar. So you'll need to replace the sugary, starchy foods in your diet with wiser choices. In the next chapter, I'll show you how.

CHAPTER 3

COOKING WITHOUT SUGAR

Healthy Alternatives to Sugar, Starches, and Unhealthy Carbs

The fact is, if you quit sugar, it will almost certainly be difficult at first, and you'll likely experience the withdrawal symptoms mentioned in chapter 1. But these symptoms won't last forever, especially when you replace sugar with truly nutritious ingredients and use healthy alternatives to sweeten your food. Still, the less sweet food you consume—even if it is sweetened with natural, sugar-free sweeteners—the better.

Believe it or not, by constantly reducing sugar and sweeteners, your taste buds will soon get used to less-sweet flavors. (If you can't quit sugar cold turkey, you might want to replace the sugar with natural sweeteners. Once you don't crave sweetness anymore, reduce the amount of those natural sweeteners as well.) But what are those healthy alternatives? Let's take a look.

Artificial Sweeteners

First, though, I want to say a few words about artificial sweeteners, the darlings of the food industry. Artificial sweeteners such as aspartame, sucralose, or acesulfame potassium are liberally used in diet sodas and other sugar-free products. They're promoted as healthy alternatives to sugary products because the food industry has finally started to understand that people are concerned about their sugar consumption and want healthier alternatives. How healthy are these artificial sweeteners, though?

The short answer is not very. First, artificial sweeteners trick your brain. Natural sugars, such as table sugar, fructose, lactose, and glucose, bind to both of the two existing subunits of the sweet receptors in your brain. When this happens, it stimulates neurotransmitters to send signals to your brain that immediately sing "sweet!" which then signals the reward pathway of the brain. When you eat artificial sweeteners, these chemical molecules trick your sweet taste buds by stimulating *part of* the receptors. So, instead of being a perfect lock-and-key match, as with natural sugars, artificial sweeteners are only a partial match. They fit part of the structure of the sweet receptor, but not all of it. Thus you can think of artificial sweeteners

as the generic keys that thieves sometimes use to pick locks. They fit the lock just enough to allow the thief to jimmy it the rest of the way open.

It's possible that artificial sweeteners not only trick the taste buds in our mouth, but also trick our entire digestive systems—at least to some degree. If this is true—and the most recent papers on the subject indicate that it may be—then it could explain how artificial sweeteners are thought to actually *cause*, not prevent, diabetes, weight gain, and other metabolic issues. However, we may already be seeing the end result, with obesity levels and the incidence of type 2 diabetes skyrocketing at the same time that artificial sweeteners were greatly increased in our food supply. The final verdict is to avoid artificial sweeteners completely.

Stevia

Here's the first example of a safe, natural sweetener. Native to Paraguay and some parts of Brazil, this unassuming little herb has tender leaves that are ten to fifteen times sweeter than sugar—yet there are zero calories in stevia, and it does not raise blood glucose levels. Though Western cultures have only begun to fully embrace the glories of the stevia plant, the indigenous peoples of South America have used it for medicinal purposes and to sweeten drinks for more than a thousand years.

What makes stevia leaves so sweet? We have the chemicals glycosides to thank. Glycosides consist of sugar molecules that are attached to nonsugar molecules: They are part glucose and part something else. However, because the glucose is bound to something else, the human body does not metabolize it as a sugar (or even recognize it as a food), although it does metabolize the powerful antioxidants found in it. It has zero calories and will not be stored as fat weight.

When you buy stevia, look for crude stevia or crude stevia extract, which is dried whole leaf stevia with nothing else added. Avoid stevia powder; it's so easy for the manufacturer to cut it with inferior and unhealthy substances such as maltodextrin (or worse), even if it's not labeled as such. If you buy whole leaf stevia, you can easily see whether it contains nothing but actual dried stevia leaves.

Liquid stevia extracts made from stevia leaves are also handy options for a low-sugar lifestyle, and they are used in the recipes in this book. They're easier to use than stevia powder, too. When buying liquid stevia (extract), be sure to choose as natural and unprocessed a product as possible because there is a lot of variation among products and brands. Look carefully also at the dosage: Some of the stevia extracts are very concentrated, while others are more diluted. Many liquid stevias contain alcohol, though in negligible amounts. If you want to choose alcohol-free stevia, go for stevia glycerite.

Then there are flavored stevias, which offer a whole world of taste. From vanilla to cinnamon, and from English toffee to Valencia orange—and even dark chocolate!—there's sure to be one that appeals to you. Just remember to read the label. Choose natural products, and leave ones with suspicious ingredients on the shelf.

Erythritol

Erythritol, a sugar alcohol, is another wholesome sweetener. Naturally occurring in some fruits and fermented foods, it's become a popular sweetener in low-carb and low-sugar baking, thanks to its pure, sweet taste and because it's easy to tolerate. Some people complain about its cooling aftertaste, but most get used to the taste of erythritol relatively easily. When it's combined with other sweeteners such as stevia, the aftertaste can be avoided or at least reduced.

Unlike many other sugar alcohols, erythritol has hardly any calories. It doesn't promote tooth decay, so you can use it in desserts or add it to coffee. It doesn't cause upset stomachs as easily as other sugar alcohols, which trigger bloating and diarrhea for sensitive people. Also, diabetics can use erythritol freely because it doesn't increase blood sugar levels (as with any food, individual reactions may vary). If you are one of the rare people who get an upset stomach or high blood glucose levels from erythritol, choose another sweetener, such as stevia or monk fruit.

There are many different erythritol products on the market. There are also sweeteners containing both erythritol and stevia, in which erythritol is the bulk ingredient and stevia gives the final sweet touch. The sweetness of erythritol is about 60 to 70 percent of the sweetness of table sugar, so you need more of it to achieve the same sweetness. When you wean yourself off sugar and its overtly sweet taste, that 60 to 70 percent sweetness should be plenty. Naturally, you can even reduce the amount further; the ultimate goal is to get rid of all added sweetness.

Choosing high-quality erythritol pays off: You'll get the best flavor with as little aftertaste as possible. This is especially true for powdered erythritol because in cold dishes such as jams and marmalades, a good-quality finely powdered erythritol doesn't crystallize, but stays well-dissolved in the food, while coarse erythritol might crystallize into an unappetizingly gritty texture. If you have a high-speed blender, you can make powdered erythritol at home from erythritol crystals. In less than a minute, you'll get a fine powder that you can use in drinks, baking, and cold desserts. There are also great erythritol-based brown sugar substitutes that have almost the same qualities as regular brown sugar, minus the calories.

When baking with erythritol, you might notice that your muffins and breads get hard on the surface. If this bothers you, reduce the amount of erythritol and supplement it with stevia. But this crystallization comes in handy when making cookies: When you take them out of the oven they're soft, but they become deliciously crunchy and crispy once cool. (Check out the Crunchy One-Bowl, Five-Ingredient Cookies on page 164.) Erythritol also helps the cookies bind together—which is great news if you don't tolerate eggs.

Check the origins of your erythritol, too, as many are made from GMO corn. (The food industry tries to fool you here as well!) Organic, non-GMO erythritol is the best choice, preferably from a well trusted brand. If you buy online, read the reviews first.

Dairy Products

When we're talking about natural sweeteners, we have to consider dairy products as well because they naturally contain lactose—milk sugar—even if they don't have any added sugar. You can enjoy dairy products on a low-sugar lifestyle when you know which ones to choose. (Of course, if dairy upsets your system, you should avoid it at all costs.)

Generally, the more fat a liquid milk product has, the lower it will be in lactose. Low- and nonfat milks have the most; half-and-half usually has less than whole milk; and whipping cream will have less still. (Do avoid half-and-half because of all the additives it contains!) Buttermilk has less lactose than plain milk, but still a fair amount. Yogurt and other partially fermented milk products such as kefir or cultured sour cream contain a fair amount of lactose, but far less than regular milk. Butter and soft cheeses contain small amounts. Hard cheeses contain only traces of lactose, so many lactose-intolerant people can enjoy these even though they can't consume other dairy products.

As for cream cheese, the good news is that it's very low in sugar. (Just avoid additives such as carrageenan; go organic and clean instead.) Surprise your guests with the Five-Ingredient Heaven and Hell Cheesecake on page 158. They'll never guess it's sugar-free! Or for a completely novel use of cream cheese, try the Two-Ingredient Crackers on page 148, which are delicious, starch-free crackers made from cream cheese and almond flour.

What about butter? For years, this healthy, natural fat has been neglected, or even banned, thanks to the low-fat craze of the 1990s. Today, we know that saturated fats don't cause heart disease, so it's fine to consume and use it in cooking and baking.

Still, times have changed when it comes to butter. The best butter is hormone- and antibiotic-free, and comes from grass-fed cows—but any butter is better than highly processed vegetable oils.

Healthy Alternatives to Starchy Flours in Cooking and Baking

Before we investigate healthy alternatives to wheat flour and other regularly used starchy flours, let's talk about the harm that starch-filled grains and other plants can do to our systems.

Plants and Their Toxic Substances

Grains such as wheat, rye, and barley contain not only sugar in the form of starch, but other substances, such as proteins that might not get absorbed completely by your digestive system, causing inflammation. Moreover, modern, highly cultivated grains have almost nothing to do with the early varieties we ate thousands of years ago—or even just a hundred years ago. In recent years, crop yield and disease resistance have taken precedence over nutrient content and digestibility when it comes to cultivating grains.

Let's not forget other starchy foods, namely pseudo-cereals and legumes. Grains such as quinoa and amaranth and legumes such as beans get a lot of good press, but is it all true? Their nutrients (which you can easily get from starch-free sources) come with the cost of lectins, phytates, and other substances that may shake your system. Plus, cereals and grains contain phytates and phytic acid which, when used liberally, can prevent absorption of important minerals including zinc, iron, and calcium. If you suffer from health conditions, especially autoimmune diseases, it's best to avoid grains and legumes altogether.

Still there are plenty of healthy, starch-free options for cooking and baking on a low-sugar lifestyle. Let's explore them!

Almond Flour

Almond flour is a staple in gluten-free, reduced-sugar baking. No wonder. Almonds are very nutritious, and with almond flour you can easily bake sweet or savory muffins, cakes, and breads. There are different types of almond flours on the market, with the most commonly used version made from blanched almonds. The taste is neutral, but it's obviously not as nutritious as almond flour made from whole almonds.

However, it still beats any starchy flour with flying colors—even gluten-free ones. If we compare 3.5 ounces (100 g) of rice flour—one of the most commonly used ingredients in commercial gluten-free products—and 3.5 ounces (100 g) of almonds, it becomes obvious that rice flour contains only minuscule amounts of nutrients. (Where that quantity of rice flour contains just 76 mg potassium, the same amount of almonds contains 733 mg potassium—ten times more!) Where rice flour contains 10 mg calcium, almonds have a whopping 269 mg calcium per 3.5 ounces (100 g). Ultimately, almonds and almond flour are much more nutritious.

Some brands of almond flour are pretty coarse (more meal than flour), while others are very fine powders. There are no standards for almond flour, and even within one brand, the quality can vary from one batch to another. In this book, I use a pretty coarse type of almond meal or flour, so the very fine-textured varieties might not work as well here, though you can certainly experiment with them. (If you're using very fine almond flour, a good rule of thumb is to use half as much as the recipe calls for.)

Coconut Flour

Coconut flour is another staple in your gluten-free, low-sugar kitchen. It's also nutritious and fiber-rich, containing minerals such as magnesium, potassium, and phosphorus as well as trace minerals such as zinc, manganese, and selenium. Plus, it's a whopping 40 percent fiber. (Whole wheat flour has about 11 percent fiber, so if anyone tries to tell you that you need grains to get your fiber, show them these staggering figures.)

Unlike almond flour, coconut flour absorbs enormous amounts of fluid. This actually makes it more affordable than almond flour, and coconut flour is already pretty cheap compared with almond flour. If a recipe calls for 1 cup (96 g) of almond flour, you can often replace it with just ¼ cup (32 g) of coconut flour. Just remember to add enough fluid, or the result may be too dry and crumbly. When it comes to coconut flour, fluid is the bulk ingredient. Remember—eggs count as a fluid, and coconut flour *needs* eggs. Otherwise, baked goods won't hold together.

The coconut flour used in the recipes in this book is very fine, just like wheat flour. Always choose the finest, whitest coconut flour with as little odor as possible for the best, most neutral-tasting result.

Psyllium Husk Powder

Consisting mostly of soluble fiber, psyllium husks have been used for decades to treat different stomach ailments—constipation and diarrhea alike. (Psyllium is a gentle, natural bulk laxative: If you've ever had Metamucil, you've already consumed it, because Metamucil *is* psyllium.) They come in whole husks, in powdered form, and in a version that's somewhere in between. Always choose the powdered form for baking—or, if you can't find it, grind whole husks into powder with a mortar and pestle. Psyllium is a great tool when it comes to healthy, starch-free baking because it improves texture, making baked goods rise remarkably well and helping them bind together. So if you have trouble with crumbly baked goods that break easily, add some psyllium husk powder next time. A little goes a long way, though, and don't forget to add fluid as well: My experiments in the kitchen suggest that each teaspoon of psyllium requires an additional scant half-cup (100 ml) of fluid. The typical amount used in recipes varies from a pinch to a few tablespoons (27 g).

Psyllium also makes a perfect egg replacement for those who can't tolerate eggs. My Savory Ricotta Butternut Squash Tart on page 118 is a good example of how egg can easily be replaced with psyllium.

Chia Seeds

Chia seeds, which come from the *Salvia hispanica* plant, are wildly popular among health enthusiasts these days, thanks to their numerous health benefits and deliciously crunchy texture. But they're not a modern invention. Ancient populations such as the Mayans and Aztecs consumed them in great quantities, too. Chia seeds are still used in their native environments—Argentina, Bolivia, Guatemala, Mexico, and Paraguay—in foods and drinks.

Miniature nutritional powerhouses, chia seeds contain lots of minerals including magnesium, manganese, calcium, phosphorus, zinc, and potassium. They're also rich in thiamine (vitamin B_1), riboflavin (vitamin B_2), niacin (vitamin B_3), and antioxidants, and are a great source of dietary fiber. Like psyllium, chia seeds also absorb unbelievable amounts of fluid: ten times their own weight, to be exact. So they're great for baking or for oh-so-trendy chia puddings. If you're not a fan of their texture, never fear, you can use milled chia seeds instead.

Almond Butters and Nut Butters

Nut butters are a great resource for healthy, low-sugar, starch-free baking. Almond and other nut butters have nothing to do with dairy-based butter; they're simply nuts that have been so finely ground that they've formed a thick paste (and sometimes oil is added to help processing).

You can buy commercially made nut butters, but watch out because some contain sugar. It's just as easy to make almond butter yourself if you have a high-speed blender and a suitable jar. Just blend raw or toasted almonds or other nuts into a smooth paste. Add extra-light olive oil or extra-virgin coconut oil little by little while blending if the mixture becomes too thick. Transfer to a jar and store in the fridge for up to two weeks.

Experiment with different nut butters, for example cashew butter, sunflower butter, macadamia butter, sesame butter (tahini), hazelnut butter, and ever-popular peanut butter. (A note on peanut butter, though: It should be used only in small amounts due to its significant carb content, and you should avoid if completely if you're allergic to peanuts.) All of these are great ingredients for low-sugar baking, and I use them liberally in the recipes in this book.

Grass-Fed Whey Protein

Athletes have relied on whey protein powders for ages—and no wonder because whey protein quickly replenishes your glycogen (muscle starch!) supplies after exercise. And it's a complete protein, too.

What are the benefits of using whey protein in baking? Well, whey protein improves the texture of baked goods remarkably. It helps them rise and bind together, and imparts a relatively dense but moist texture. It produces especially good results when it's used in "large" baked goods, such as breads and cakes—like my Easy Fluffy Bread on page 53.

Opt for high-quality whey protein made from grass-fed cows. Grass-fed whey protein has four times more omega-3 fatty acids than grain-fed whey protein. It's also rich in CLA (conjugated linoleic acid), which aids fat burning; plus immunoglobulins, which help your body fight viruses and bacteria; and lactoferrin, which helps normalize your iron levels. Besides, grain-fed cows are given pesticides, antibiotics, and even hormones to prevent illness and stimulate milk production—and that's never a good thing. (Avoid those with added sugars, though those made with stevia are fine).

Egg White Protein

Egg white protein—which is basically just dried, powdered egg white—is great for low-sugar baking. Like whey protein, egg white protein has a complete amino acid profile. When used in baking, egg white protein helps baked goods rise and bind together. Because of these qualities, egg white protein performs best in breads, and you have to be careful not to use too much, or the result could be dry and leathery. Ideally, it should be combined with other types of protein, such as whey protein or plant-based protein. (My experiments show that half egg white protein and half whey protein produces the best result.)

Plant-Based Proteins

If you can't tolerate dairy or eggs, plant-based proteins are your best bet. Rice protein—when made from sprouted brown rice—is the most nutritious plant-based protein. Soy protein isolate is also a complete protein, but I avoid soy, so I can't really speak for it. Plus, because it can be tough on the stomach, many people experience gas and bloating when they consume it. Rice protein, on the other hand, is the best-tolerated plant-based protein, and the most gentle on the stomach.

Rice, hemp, and pea proteins also have benefits for starch-free baking, though the effects are milder. Breads made with them won't rise as high, and are crumblier. Also, these plant-based proteins, especially hemp protein, tend to lend a green color to baked goods (perfect for Halloween or St. Patrick's Day, perhaps?). Hemp and pea proteins may cause stomach upset in some people, and they usually lack some essential amino acids. They do contain more natural sugars than whey protein or egg white protein.

So if you want to choose a plant-based protein, rice protein made from sprouted brown rice is the best option, in both nutrients and tolerance level. Just make sure that they contain only natural ingredients, and that only stevia is used if they are sweetened.

Starch-Free Alternatives to Pasta, Rice, and Potatoes

With a little imagination, many nonstarchy vegetables can be used in lieu of pasta, rice, and potatoes. Cauliflower, for instance, is a longtime low-carb staple, replacing potato and rice. These days, you can buy cauliflower rice in some stores, but it's easy to make at home, too, by processing chunks of cauliflower into a rice-like consistency in your food processor, and using it in place of regular starchy rice. You can prepare risottos with it (try the Easy Cauli Rice Mushroom and Parmesan Risotto on page 142); you can use it in paellas, such as the Cauli Rice Seafood Paella on page 139; and it makes a great side dish, as in the Vegetarian Eggplant Curry with Cauli Basmati Rice on page 136. When cooking cauliflower rice, it's best to leave it al dente, or crisp-tender.

Spiralized zucchini (zoodles, or zucchini noodles) and other spiralized nonstarchy vegetables make perfect pasta substitutes. There are fancy spiralizer machines on the market, but you don't really have to buy one. A good old grater will do the job very well. (A food processor with a grating blade works perfectly, too.) One of the great advantages of using spiralized vegetables is that you don't have to cook them: Just add them raw to the dish in the end. Make a perfect, low-carb lunch or dinner by topping an ample amount of spiralized vegetables with a hearty, creamy sauce.

Thanks to its low sugar content, spaghetti squash—nature's own starch-free spaghetti—has also become a low-carb favorite, and can be used in place of regular spaghetti in various dishes. Plus, you don't have to grate or spiralize anything: Just scoop the strands, or "spaghetti," out of the cooked squash!

Turnip and rutabaga are nutritious, low-starch options, too, and even make great "French fries." Just toss them in extra-light olive oil, spices, and salt, then bake them in the oven.

Shirataki Pasta

At health food stores or online, you can find shirataki, or "miracle," noodles (and rice), which is made from glucomannan, a natural dietary water-soluble fiber that the human body cannot digest. Glucomannan contains hardly any calories, and it may have several health benefits: It's been used to treat constipation, improve blood lipid profile, and increase insulin sensitivity in type 2 diabetics. Serve shirataki pasta or rice topped with scrumptious, low-sugar sauces, or as a side dish. If you can't find them, replace them in the recipes in this book with zoodles or other spiralized nonstarchy vegetables.

Starch-Free Thickeners

Gelatin is a perfect starch-free thickener, and it has great health benefits, too: It's alleged to help ease arthritis, leaky gut, food allergies, skin problems, and candida infections. In this book, I use gelatin to thicken Low-Sugar Orange Marmalade (page 48), and in my kid-pleasing Sugar-Free Natural-Ingredient Gummy Bears (page 168).

Another starch-free—and nearly calorie-free—thickener is glucomannan powder. Remember those shirataki noodles? Well, this is the same stuff, just in powder form. When thickening recipes with glucomannan, know that a little goes a long way because it absorbs enormous amounts of water. Be sure to add it pinch by pinch. My recipe for Homemade Sugar-Free Maple Syrup on page 52 is a good example of how to use glucomannan powder.

If you can't find glucomannan, look for guar gum or xanthan gum, both of which are also whitish powders. Guar gum is the ground inner part of guar beans, while xanthan gum is secreted by a bacterium, *Xanthomonas campestris*, from sugar substrates. Both guar gum and xanthan gum are polysaccharides, but they are soluble fibers that your body cannot break down. Xanthan gum is widely used in gluten-free baking as a binding agent, and to improve texture. Like glucomannan, a little goes a long way: You'll probably use somewhere between a fraction of a teaspoon and one teaspoon in a recipe. Avoid lumps by sprinkling them in little by little, mixing well as you do so. I use xanthan gum in my Low-Sugar Sweet and Sour Sauce on page 38 and in my Easy Sugar-Free Strawberry Jam on page 51.

Other Healthy Ingredients for Low-Sugar Cooking

Low-sugar cooking is easy when your pantry is stocked properly. Here are low-carb staples that'll add flavor and cut cooking time—without sacrificing taste or health benefits.

Spices and Seasonings

When you're making food from scratch, having spice and seasoning mixes on hand is a great help—but lots of store-bought seasoning mixes contain food additives and starches (plus refined salt). Use salt-free spice seasoning mixes, and stick to natural salts such as unrefined sea salt and Himalayan salt, which contain minerals (and taste better, too).

Natural Flavorings and Extracts

Most flavorings and extracts on the market are artificial, but you can find natural flavorings if you look for them. They're especially useful for desserts: Take vanilla, for instance, which turns up in countless treats. And because of its naturally sweet flavor, you'll be able to use less sweetener in your recipe. Vanilla beans are wonderful for custards and puddings, and powdered vanilla bean is delicious in everything from baked goods to chilled or frozen creations, such as puddings and ice creams. Be sure to choose clean, organic, sugar-free versions—and alcohol-free, glycerine-based extract or flavoring is the best choice for kids.

Countless other flavorings and extracts are available, too. Again, avoid those with suspicious chemicals (for instance, propylene glycol is, terrifyingly, used in antifreeze substances) or close-to-poisonous colors (Red 40, or allura red AC, causes ADHD-like behavior in children). Choose only sugar-free extracts with natural flavor sources.

Essential Oils

Did you know that you can use essential oils in cooking? Citrus essential oils in particular, such as orange oil, lend a powerful, brisk, fruity note to your dishes without the added sugar in whole fruit. (My Low-Sugar Orange Marmalade on page 48 is a great example.) Always be sure to choose food-grade essential oil, and be aware that the oils are so strong that a single drop—or two at most—is enough. Never, ever add more, or you might damage your intestines.

Dark Chocolate and Dark Cocoa Powder

Great news for chocolate lovers: Chocolate is actually a health food! There are loads of antioxidants and nutrients in unsweetened dark cocoa powder and dark chocolate with a minimum cocoa content of 85 percent. Studies have shown that dark chocolate can prevent cardiovascular disease (CVD), improve brain function, and lower high blood pressure. So feel free to enjoy it—in moderation, of course.

A Word About Protein

Unlike carbohydrate consumption, eating protein is absolutely essential to human life. We simply cannot survive long-term without eating protein because our bodies cannot synthesize the amino acids we need to survive. Therefore, we have to get essential amino acids from the protein in our diets.

Still, it's also true that too much protein can adversely affect your health in very serious and significant ways. Eating too much protein raises blood glucose levels through gluconeogenesis, which is the breakdown of amino acids into glucose in the liver and kidneys. Gluconeogenesis causes insulin levels to rise significantly in order to compensate for this extra sugar. Though this extra insulin can lower your blood sugar over the short-term, it causes insulin resistance—that is, type 2 diabetes—in the long run.

Also, eating excess protein can lead to a chronic rise in leptin, or the satiety hormone. In the same way that too much insulin leads cell membranes to become insulin resistant, chronically high levels of leptin cause the receptors on your hypothalamus to become resistant to leptin. This can lead to fat storage and food cravings—which, in turn, encourages you to eat more and to store more fat, which leads to more leptin resistance, causing a vicious cycle that's difficult to break. Consuming high levels of protein can also accelerate aging and increases the risk of cancer.

So how much protein do you need to consume each day in order to supply your body with the essential amino acids it needs? For an average healthy, moderately active person, target protein consumption should be about 0.7 to 1 gram of protein per kilogram of *lean* body mass. Lean body mass includes the mass of your muscles, bones, organs, and tendons, but excludes your body fat. So, your lean body mass is simply your total weight minus your body fat. Because it's hard to know exactly how much body fat you have, you can use simple estimates instead. You'll easily find online calculators that'll help you calculate your lean body mass.

If you are diabetic, you may want to reduce your daily protein intake a little more. Ron Rosedale, M.D., a well-known advocate of a low-carb, moderate-protein diet, states that he first puts his diabetic patients on a carbohydrate-restricted diet. However, if their blood sugar doesn't decrease sufficiently, his next step is to put them on a protein-restricted diet of 0.5 to 0.7 gram of protein per kilogram of lean body mass. Rosedale reports very good results with this method: His patients' blood sugar levels stabilize, their blood lipid profiles improve, metabolic issues are resolved, and blood pressure is normalized.

A Word About Fat

You might be asking yourself, "If I have to restrict my sugar—that is, carbohydrate— intake *and* restrict my protein intake, what *can* I eat?!" Here's the answer: Increase your consumption of *healthy* fats from minimally processed whole foods, such as seeds, nuts, nut butters; plus the natural fat in fish, grass-fed beef, free-range pasture-fed chicken and eggs; and cold-pressed olive, avocado, and coconut oils—and grass-fed butter, which is an especially excellent natural fat. (This does not include hydrogenated or partially hydrogenated oils, which are the unhealthy trans-fats that are so abundant in processed foods, nor does it include any fats that have been overly processed.)

Memorize this important fact: Fat is actually good for you! So much misinformation on fat abounds that you might have to spend some time reprogramming your brain in order to believe it. The truth is that we need fat for thousands of vital bodily functions. From every cell membrane to the white matter in our brains, from absorbing fat-soluble vitamins to synthesizing hormones, fat is present—and necessary—throughout our bodies. Without it, we would die.

This is true only for natural fats, though— the fats we have consumed since the dawn of the human race. This doesn't apply to highly processed vegetable seed oils, which are highly toxic. They oxidize (that is, become rancid) when heated, creating carcinogenic compounds and causing inflammation. So stay away from vegetable seed oils such as canola, sunflower, safflower, soybean, corn, cottonseed, and rapeseed. The best fats for cooking are saturated fats. Coconut oil is the absolute best, followed by lard and other animal fats, such as butter: They're the most stable, and don't become rancid when heated. Olive oil and avocado oil can be also used for cooking, as they contain mainly monounsaturated fatty acids, which don't break that easily—though they're still more unstable than saturated fats and are best used in salad dressings and other cold dishes.

The myth that saturated fats cause CVD has finally been debunked, so we can finally accept that it isn't fat we need to fear: It's sugar. So let's ditch the fat phobia, and welcome healthy fats back into our diets. The recipes in this book will encourage you to do just that—and they'll keep you nourished and satisfied so that your body and mind can thrive.

CHAPTER 4

BASICS & PANTRY STAPLES

It's normal to feel overwhelmed when you're starting a low-sugar lifestyle, and you might have a lot of questions about it. What can you eat, and what's off-limits? Which ingredients should you choose? How do you prepare low-sugar food that's both nutritious and delicious?

Well, this chapter is here to help. It's full of low-sugar recipes for the staples you'll be using again and again, so that you'll always have healthy ingredients on hand, and won't have to reach for sugar-laden processed stuff in a pinch. (Plus, the homemade versions taste better.)

So, whether you're looking for sugar-free ketchup (a guaranteed kid-pleaser!), easy-to-make mayo, guilt-free jams and marmalades, or fluffy, sliceable starch-free bread, you're sure to find inspiration in the pages that follow.

LOW-SUGAR SWEET AND SOUR SAUCE

Commercial sweet and sour sauce easily contains more than 30 percent sugar, but this flavorful, homemade version has ten times less! Better yet, this exceptionally simple and seriously good condiment is ready in no time: Just mix all the ingredients together and heat until thick. Use it as a wok sauce for Asian-style dishes, in the Easy Breakfast Burrito on page 85, or serve it as a condiment with chicken or vegetable dishes. It also makes a great dip for starch-free crackers and raw vegetables.

Yield: about 1¾ cups (410 ml)

Place the water, erythritol, vinegar, tomato paste, soy sauce, stevia, and salt in a small saucepan and whisk well. Sprinkle in the xanthan while constantly whisking. Place the saucepan over a high heat, constantly mixing. When the mixture starts to thicken—and before it begins to boil—remove it from the heat. Let cool to room temperature before refrigerating. Store in an airtight container in the fridge. The sauce tastes best the following day, after the flavors have had time to combine. Use within two weeks.

INGREDIENTS

⅔ cup (160 ml) water

½ cup (65 g) powdered erythritol

3 tablespoons (45 ml) rice vinegar

3 tablespoons (48 g) unsweetened tomato paste

1½ tablespoons (25 ml) naturally fermented gluten-free soy sauce, such as tamari

15 drops liquid stevia, or to taste

¼ teaspoon unrefined sea salt or Himalayan salt, or to taste

½ teaspoon xanthan gum

TIP: If you don't have rice vinegar, use raw apple cider vinegar or another mild-tasting vinegar instead.

NUTRITION INFO

IN TOTAL:

3.3 g protein;
0.4 g fat;
12.2 g net carbs;
66 kcal

PER TABLESPOON (15 ML):

0.1 g protein;
trace fat;
0.5 g net carbs;
3 kcal

FIVE-INGREDIENT SUGAR-FREE KETCHUP

This is every parent's dream: super-healthy, sugar-free ketchup! Made with an erythritol-based brown sugar substitute that is almost noncaloric, it's a healthy condiment that's delicious for dipping low-carb rutabaga or turnip fries, or the Easy Broccoli "Tater Tots" on page 147. Remember that placing the ketchup mixture over a higher heat causes it to thicken faster—but it does splatter easily, so take care and keep a lid handy while cooking.

INGREDIENTS

2 cups (450 g) unsweetened tomato sauce

¼ cup (40 g) erythritol-based brown sugar substitute

2 tablespoons (28 ml) raw apple cider vinegar

⅛ teaspoon Ceylon cinnamon

Pinch of cayenne pepper

Yield: about 2 cups (450 g)

Place all the ingredients in a medium saucepan over a high heat and bring to a boil. Reduce the heat to medium and boil, uncovered, until the ketchup has reached the desired consistency (about 30 minutes), stirring every 5 minutes. As the ketchup thickens, it may splatter, so be careful. If so, reduce the heat and cover the saucepan with a lid until the splattering stops. Let cool to room temperature before refrigerating. Store in an airtight container in the fridge, and use within one week.

NO-SUGAR TERIYAKI SAUCE

NOTE: If you prefer a thicker sauce, sprinkle ½ teaspoon xanthan gum or glucomannan into the mixture before heating. Whisk carefully when adding the thickener to prevent lumps.

Traditional Japanese teriyaki sauce is sweet and tangy, but commercial versions often contain a huge amount of sugar, which can be responsible for as much one-third of their total calorie count. This guilt-free version, however, has no added sugar. Instead, it gets its sweetness from an erythritol-based brown sugar substitute, which is almost calorie-free. It's easy to adjust the level of sweetness to your taste.

Yield: about 1 cup (240 ml)

Place all ingredients in a small saucepan and bring to a boil over a high heat, mixing constantly. Once boiling, remove from the heat and let cool to room temperature. Use it just like traditional teriyaki sauce— to make teriyaki chicken, for example, or the Terrific Teriyaki Pork Sandwich on page 108.

INGREDIENTS

½ cup (120 ml) naturally fermented gluten-free soy sauce, such as tamari

⅓ cup (53 g) erythritol-based brown sugar substitute

¼ cup (60 ml) dry sherry

¼ cup (60 ml) rice vinegar

1 teaspoon ground ginger

¼ teaspoon garlic powder

TIP: If you want to use fresh ingredients, replace the garlic powder with 1 minced garlic clove and replace the ground ginger with 1 tablespoon (8 g) of grated ginger root.

NUTRITION INFO

IN TOTAL:

12.3 g protein;
0.3 g fat;
8.8 g net carbs;
154 kcal

PER TABLESPOON (15 ML):

0.6 g protein;
trace fat;
0.5 g net carbs;
8 kcal

FOOLPROOF ONE-MINUTE MAYO

Think it's hard to make homemade mayonnaise? Think again. This is the quickest, easiest way to prepare mayonnaise, ever, and it's healthy as well because it calls for light olive oil instead of unhealthy, omega-6-filled canola or sunflower oil. (Light olive oil is more neutral-tasting than extra-virgin, which might be too strong for mayonnaise.) This simple mayo is used in lots of recipes in this book, so be sure to keep a batch on hand. (Note that this recipe contains raw egg.)

INGREDIENTS

1 very fresh egg

2 teaspoons unsweetened mustard (such as Dijon)

⅛ teaspoon ground white pepper

¼ teaspoon unrefined sea salt or Himalayan salt, or to taste

2 teaspoons raw apple cider vinegar

¾ cup (180 ml) extra-light olive oil

Yield: about 1 cup (225 g)

1. Place the egg, mustard, white pepper, salt, and vinegar into a deep, narrow blending jar. Then insert an immersion blender into the jar so that it reaches the bottom.

2. Now pour in the olive oil. Don't lift the immersion blender or turn it on yet: Let it stand in the bottom of the jar, covering the egg and the other ingredients.

3. Start blending on the highest speed. Blend until the oil is completely incorporated and the mayonnaise is smooth. (You can lift the blender very slowly at the end of the process to make sure all the oil is incorporated.) This phase shouldn't take longer than a minute. Store the finished mayonnaise in the fridge for up to two days.

NOTE: You can also prepare the mayonnaise in the traditional way by adding the oil little by little to the rest of the ingredients, beating vigorously all the time with a whisk or electric mixer.

FANTASTIC FRENCH DRESSING

Here's another classic low-carb dressing that combines great taste and good fats. And its sharp yet sophisticated flavor is a perfect match for the Greek Salad with Chicken and Strawberries on page 101, or similarly fruity-yet-savory salads. If you prefer your dressing on the sweet side, add a couple of drops of liquid stevia to the mix.

Yield: about 6 tablespoons (95 ml)

1. Place all the ingredients in a small jar with a tight-fitting lid. Close the lid tightly and shake vigorously until the mixture is smooth. For best results, let the flavors mingle for a few hours before serving.

2. Store in the fridge and bring to room temperature 30 minutes before use. Shake well before serving.

INGREDIENTS

1 tablespoon (15 ml) freshly squeezed lemon juice

⅓ cup (80 ml) extra-virgin olive oil

¼ teaspoon mustard powder

1 garlic clove, crushed

Pinch unrefined sea salt or Himalayan salt

NUTRITION INFO

IN TOTAL:
0.5 g protein;
73.5 g fat;
0.8 g net carbs;
666 kcal

PER TABLESPOON (16 ML):
0.1 g protein;
12.2 g fat;
0.1 g net carbs;
111 kcal

NUTRITION INFO

IN TOTAL:
0.4 g protein;
82.3 g fat;
1.6 g net carbs;
749 kcal

PER TABLESPOON (15 ML):
trace protein;
8.2 g fat;
0.2 g net carbs;
75 kcal

QUICK RASPBERRY VINAIGRETTE

This flavorful, easy-to-make vinaigrette adds a dash of elegance to just about any salad, and it's also a delicious way to add extra vitamins and healthy fats to your diet—minus the nasty sugar and its harmful effects, of course. Use a high-speed blender to break up the gritty seeds and to achieve a smooth, rich result. Feel free to experiment with other berries here, too, such as strawberries and blueberries.

INGREDIENTS

¼ cup (25 g) fresh raspberries, or thawed frozen raspberries

2 tablespoons (28 ml) raw apple cider vinegar

6 tablespoons (90 ml) extra-virgin olive oil

5 drops liquid stevia, or to taste

¼ teaspoon unrefined sea salt or Himalayan salt, or to taste

Yield: about ⅔ cup (160 ml)

Simply place all the ingredients in a high-speed blender and blend until smooth. Serve immediately, or store in an airtight container in the fridge and bring to room temperature 30 minutes before use. Shake well before serving.

NOTE: To make this recipe even simpler, make a batch of the Easy Sugar-Free Strawberry Jam recipe on page 51 ahead of time, replacing the strawberries with raspberries. Then, to make this vinaigrette, just replace the raspberries and stevia with 2 tablespoons (30 g) of the jam.

NUTRITION INFO

IN TOTAL:
57.0 g protein;
150.5 g fat;
30.4 g net carbs;
1704 kcal

PER ¼ CUP (60 ML):
7.1 g protein;
18.8 g fat;
3.8 g net carbs;
213 kcal

SIMPLE AND SUCCULENT SATAY SAUCE

Full of richness and exotic flavor, this Thai-style satay sauce is ready in mere minutes. Enjoy it warm with chicken, fish, or vegetable dishes, and don't forget to add chopped salted peanuts before serving: They enhance the flavor and texture even more. If you prefer a thicker sauce, increase the amount of peanut butter; if you prefer a thinner sauce, increase the coconut milk.

Yield: about 2 cups (480 ml)

Combine all the ingredients in a small saucepan and place over high heat, stirring constantly. When the mixture is hot and smooth, remove it from the heat. Let cool slightly and serve warm, sprinkled with chopped peanuts.

INGREDIENTS

1 cup (240 ml) coconut milk

⅔ cup (160 g) crunchy unsweetened peanut butter

1½ tablespoons (23 g) sugar-free Thai red curry paste

1 to 2 tablespoons (15 to 28 ml) fish sauce

10 drops liquid stevia, or to taste

¼ cup (30 g) chopped salted peanuts, to serve

TIP: For a fruitier-tasting sauce, replace the stevia with 2 tablespoons (30 g) of Five-Ingredient Sugar-Free Ketchup (page 39).

FIVE-INGREDIENT SUGAR-FREE CHOCOLATE HAZELNUT SPREAD

Commercial chocolate hazelnut spreads contain both a good deal of sugar and processed vegetable oils, which are infamous for their inflammation-inflicting omega-6 content. But this healthy, homemade option uses only natural sweeteners and real butter, which is far heart healthier. Smear it on a slice of Easy Fluffy Bread (page 53) for a quick, light breakfast or snack.

Yield: about ¾ cup (195 g)

Combine all the ingredients in a high-speed blender and blend until a smooth paste is formed. Add more sweetener if needed, then blend well again. Store in an airtight container in the fridge and bring to room temperature 30 minutes before use. Use within one week.

INGREDIENTS

¾ cup (85 g) crushed toasted hazelnuts

¼ cup (2 ounces or 60 g) unsalted grass-fed butter, softened

1 tablespoon (7 g) unsweetened dark cocoa powder

3 tablespoons (24 g) powdered erythritol or other preferred sweetener, or to taste

2 tablespoons (28 ml) extra-light olive oil

½ teaspoon vanilla extract (optional)

NUTRITION INFO

IN TOTAL:
15.4 g protein;
130.1 g fat;
5.5 g net carbs;
1260 kcal

PER TABLESPOON (16 G):
1.1 g protein;
9.3 g fat;
0.4 g net carbs;
90 kcal

THREE-INGREDIENT SUGAR-FREE CARAMEL GLAZE

Yield: about 1 cup (240 ml)

Great news: It's possible to make a healthy, sugar-free caramel glaze with just three natural ingredients. Sound too good to be true? Well, it's not! In fact, you can make caramel using just two ingredients—heavy cream and erythritol—but the salted butter enhances its flavor and produces a perfectly glossy sauce. And the longer you cook it, the thicker your sauce will be. Try topping your favorite low-sugar desserts with this luscious treat.

1. Place the heavy cream and the sweetener in a medium saucepan and bring to a boil over a medium-high heat, stirring constantly. Reduce the heat to medium, then simmer uncovered until thick, about 15 minutes, stirring all the time. You'll know the sauce is ready when you can see the bottom of the saucepan as you whisk it. Be sure to watch the mixture constantly during cooking; it can boil over in seconds. Reduce the heat if the mixture is about to spill.

2. When the caramel is thick, remove from the heat. Add the butter and mix well, until the butter is melted and is completely incorporated into the mixture.

3. Cover and let it cool down. Use as glaze or sauce immediately, or store in the fridge in an airtight container and consume within three days.

INGREDIENTS

1½ cups (350 ml) heavy cream

3 tablespoons (30 g) erythritol-based brown sugar substitute

1 tablespoon (14 g) salted grass-fed butter

TIP: Be extremely careful with the boiling cream, as it boils over very easily. Using a larger saucepan helps prevent this, and also allows you to use a higher heat, which, in turn, reduces cooking time.

NUTRITION INFO

IN TOTAL:
7.4 g protein;
138.2 g fat;
11.7 g net carbs;
1319 kcal

PER TABLESPOON (15 ML):
0.5 g protein;
8.6 g fat;
0.7 g net carbs;
82 kcal

LOW-SUGAR ORANGE MARMALADE

Traditional orange marmalade is terribly high in sugar—but now you can enjoy all that fresh, succulent flavor without sugar and its harmful effects. Plus, this marmalade has a smooth texture, which makes it easily spreadable (and more kid-friendly). Discarding the white pith of the orange before cooking guarantees a perfectly fruity marmalade without a hint of bitterness, and long, slow cooking ensures naturally deep, sweet flavors.

INGREDIENTS

2 oranges

1 cup (240 ml) plus ¼ cup (60 ml) water divided

1 cup (130 g) powdered erythritol

40 drops orange-flavored stevia

2 teaspoons gelatin powder

2 drops 100 percent orange essential oil

Yield: about 2½ cups (750 g)

1. Wash the oranges and pat them dry. Finely grate the peel from 1 orange and place it in a medium saucepan. (Be sure to grate the orange part of the peel only and leave out the white pith: it's very bitter.)

2. Peel both oranges. Discard the peels and seeds and use only the flesh. Remove as much of the white pith as possible. Chop the flesh into ½-inch (1.3 cm) chunks. Add these to the saucepan, along with 1 cup (240 ml) of the water, the powdered erythritol, and the orange stevia. Mix well and bring to a boil over a high heat. Once boiling, reduce the heat to low. Cover, and let the mixture simmer for 3 hours.

3. When the mixture has simmered for close to 3 hours, pour the remaining ¼ cup (60 ml) water into a small cup. Sprinkle the gelatin powder on top. Let the gelatin soak and thicken for 5 minutes, then add it to the hot orange mixture and mix well until completely dissolved. Add the orange essential oil and mix again. Pour the hot marmalade into sterilized glass jars or a ceramic container. Let cool to room temperature, then refrigerate overnight. The marmalade will set in the fridge. Store in the fridge and consume within two weeks.

NUTRITION INFO

IN TOTAL:

9.7 g protein;
0.4 g fat;
31.5 g net carbs;
199 kcal

PER ¼ CUP (60 G):

1.0 g protein;
trace fat;
3.2 g net carbs;
20 kcal

PER TABLESPOON (20 G):

0.2 g protein;
trace fat;
0.8 g net carbs;
5 kcal

NUTRITION INFO

IN TOTAL:
2.3 g protein;
0.9 g fat;
38.1 g net carbs;
172 kcal

PER TABLESPOON (15 G):
0.1 g protein;
trace fat;
1.4 g net carbs;
6 kcal

EASY SUGAR-FREE STRAWBERRY JAM

You won't believe how easy it is to make homemade sugar-free strawberry jam. And you can tailor it to your taste, too: Cooking the mixture for less time yields a chunkier jam, while longer cooking results in a smoother texture and a sweeter flavor. Use this summery jam to dress up your breakfast yogurt or to accompany a sugar-free cheesecake, or slather it on a slice of starch-free peanut butter bread to make a healthy PB&J sandwich.

INGREDIENTS

1 pound (450 g) fresh strawberries, or thawed frozen strawberries

¼ cup (32 g) powdered erythritol

40 drops liquid vanilla stevia, or to taste

2 pinches xanthan gum

Yield: about 1½ cups (350 g)

1. Combine the strawberries, erythritol, and vanilla stevia in a large saucepan. Place over a high heat, stirring constantly (and scraping the bottom of the saucepan as you stir). When the mixture begins to steam, reduce the heat to low. Cook for 15 to 20 minutes, or until the mixture has reached the desired consistency. (Feel free to leave it as chunky as you like.) Mix constantly during cooking, crushing and breaking the strawberries with the back and sides of the mixing spoon.

2. Sprinkle in the xanthan gum little by little on top of the mixture, stirring all the time. (If you like, you can sift in the xanthan gum through a tea strainer to prevent lumps.) Continue mixing and let the jam simmer for 2 to 3 minutes before removing from the heat. Cover with a lid and let the jam cool completely. Store it in an airtight container in the fridge and consume within one week. You can also freeze the jam for up to two months, or preserve it for longer in sterilized glass jars.

HOMEMADE SUGAR-FREE MAPLE SYRUP

NOTE: This "maple syrup" is intentionally less sweet than regular maple syrup, to help wean you off the unnaturally sweet taste. However, if you'd like to make it sweeter, use 1 cup (240 ml) erythritol-based brown sugar substitute.

There's no need to skimp on this delicious condiment: You can happily drown your starch-free pancakes and waffles in it without worrying about the harmful sugar load that's part and parcel of traditional maple syrup. And it tastes, looks, and feels just like the real thing! I use Frontier Natural Products maple flavor for this recipe, so if you use another type of maple flavor, be sure to adjust the amount accordingly.

Yield: about 2 cups (475 ml)

1. Combine the water and the sweetener in a small saucepan and bring to a rolling boil over high heat. Mix a couple of times while heating.

2. Remove the saucepan from the heat and, very carefully, sprinkle in the glucomannan while whisking vigorously to prevent lumps. Add the maple flavoring and mix well again. Adjust the taste by adding more sweetener or maple flavoring, if necessary. Let cool to room temperature. The syrup will thicken during cooling. Pour the syrup into a glass bottle and store in the fridge for up to two weeks.

INGREDIENTS

1½ cups (350 ml) water

¾ cup (120 g) erythritol-based brown sugar substitute

½ teaspoon glucomannan

1 teaspoon sugar-free maple flavoring, or to taste

TIP: Glucomannan is the best thickener to use here because it produces the smoothest, most neutral-tasting result.

NUTRITION INFO

IN TOTAL:

0.1 g protein;
trace fat;
3.5 g net carbs;
10 kcal

PER TABLESPOON (15 ML):

trace protein;
trace fat;
0.1 g net carbs;
0 kcal

NUTRITION INFO

IN TOTAL:
84.3 g protein;
95.9 g fat;
22.6 g net carbs;
1293 kcal

PER SLICE,
IF 12 SLICES IN TOTAL:
7.0 g protein;
8.0 g fat;
1.9 g net carbs;
108 kcal

PER SLICE,
IF 24 SLICES IN TOTAL:
3.5 g protein;
4.0 g fat;
0.9 g net carbs;
54 kcal

EASY FLUFFY BREAD

In 2012, I posted my first fluffy bread recipe on my blog. Since then, I've made several improvements to the recipe, this one being the latest—and absolute best!—version. Its texture is fabulously light and fluffy, but it holds together extremely well, so slice it as thinly as you like.

INGREDIENTS

¼ cup (30 g) unflavored egg white protein powder

¼ cup (20 g) unflavored grass-fed whey protein powder

1 tablespoon (9 g) psyllium husk powder

2 teaspoons baking powder

4 eggs, separated

½ cup (120 g) unsweetened cashew butter

½ cup (120 ml) unsweetened almond milk

1 teaspoon unrefined sea salt (optional)

5 drops liquid stevia, or to taste (optional)

TIP: For even lower sugar content, replace the cashew butter with macadamia nut butter.

Yield: 1 loaf

1. Preheat the oven to 350°F (175°C). Combine the egg white protein, whey protein, psyllium husk powder, and baking powder in a small bowl. Mix well to break up any lumps.

2. In a separate bowl, beat the egg whites until stiff peaks form.

3. Combine the cashew butter and egg yolks in a large bowl and beat until well combined. Then add the almond milk and salt and stevia, if using, and beat again. Add the dry ingredients to the wet, and mix well. Fold in the egg whites and mix gently with a rubber spatula until smooth. Pour the mixture into a 9 × 5-inch (23 × 13 cm) silicone loaf pan.

4. Bake in the preheated oven for 45 minutes, or until a toothpick inserted in the center of the loaf comes out clean. Remove from the pan, let cool completely, and serve.

LOW-SUGAR CINNAMON RAISIN BREAD

Raisins are relatively high in natural sugars—but this delicious Cinnamon Raisin Bread isn't. What's the secret? Chopping the raisins into tiny pieces, which yields plenty of flavor with minimal sugar. And if you add extra cinnamon and sweetener, you'll be able to reduce the quantity of raisins even further.

INGREDIENTS

¾ cup (90 g) coconut flour

⅓ cup (45 g) finely chopped raisins

¼ cup (20 g) vanilla-flavored grass-fed whey protein powder

3 tablespoons (27 g) psyllium husk powder

2 teaspoons baking powder

2 teaspoons Ceylon cinnamon

¼ teaspoon unrefined sea salt or Himalayan salt

6 eggs

1 cup (240 ml) unsweetened almond milk

25 drops liquid stevia

TIP: For variation, add ¼ cup (75 g) Low-Sugar Orange Marmalade (page 48) to the wet ingredients.

Yield: 1 loaf

1. Preheat the oven to 350°F (175°C). Place all the dry ingredients in a medium bowl. Mix well, making sure there are no lumps.

2. Place the eggs, almond milk, and stevia in another medium bowl and whisk well. Add the dry ingredients to the wet, then mix with an electric mixer until smooth. Transfer the batter to a 9 × 5-inch (23 × 13 cm) silicone loaf pan. Use a rubber spatula to form it into a loaf shape. Bake for 60 minutes, or until a toothpick inserted in the center of the loaf comes out dry. Remove from the pan, let cool completely, and serve.

NUTRITION INFO

IN TOTAL:
81.5 g protein;
58.7 g fat;
55.6 g net carbs;
1079 kcal

PER SLICE,
IF 24 SLICES IN TOTAL:
3.4 g protein;
2.4 g fat;
2.3 g net carbs;
45 kcal

PERFECT FIVE-INGREDIENT PEANUT BUTTER BREAD

NUTRITION INFO

IN TOTAL:

93.7 g protein;
104.4 g fat;
21.1 g net carbs;
1400 kcal

PER SLICE,
IF 24 SLICES IN TOTAL:

3.9 g protein;
4.4 g fat;
0.9 g net carbs;
58 kcal

If you love peanut butter bread—and who doesn't?—but don't want your blood sugar to skyrocket, then this sugar-free version is the answer to your prayers. And it takes just five ingredients to make this starch-free, gluten-free treat. Just be sure to bake it in a silicone loaf pan to prevent the dough from sticking.

Yield: 1 loaf

INGREDIENTS

½ cup (45 g) vanilla-flavored grass-fed whey protein

2 teaspoons baking powder

½ cup (120 g) unsweetened smooth peanut butter

4 eggs

¼ cup (32 g) powdered erythritol

Pinch unrefined sea salt or Himalayan salt, if the peanut butter is not salted (optional)

1. Preheat the oven to 300°F (150°C). Place the whey protein and the baking powder in a small bowl and mix well. Set aside.

2. Place the rest of the ingredients—peanut butter, eggs, sweetener, and salt, if using—in a large bowl and beat with an electric mixer until smooth, fluffy, and bubbly, about 5 minutes. Add the whey protein mixture to the peanut butter mixture and beat again until smooth and well combined.

3. Pour the batter into a 9 × 5-inch (23 × 13 cm) silicone loaf pan and bake for 40 minutes, or until a knife inserted near the center comes out clean. Remove from the pan, let cool, and slice. Serve with Easy Sugar-Free Strawberry Jam (page 51).

NOTE: To make a PB&J loaf, add ½ cup (120 g) Easy Sugar-Free Strawberry Jam (page 51) to the batter after pouring it into the loaf pan. Use a fork to make big swirls in the batter with the jam, then bake according to the instructions above.

TWO-MINUTE MILE-HIGH ENGLISH MUFFIN IN A MUG

A few basic ingredients and a couple of minutes are all you need to whip up a low-sugar English muffin that's the perfect vehicle for just about any kind of topping, such as salad, meat, eggs, cheese, or veggies. Or, for an elegant-yet-filling weekend treat, try filling it with lox, cream cheese, dill, and red onion. You won't even miss the bagel!

INGREDIENTS

Softened butter (for greasing the mug)

¼ cup (30 g) almond flour

1 teaspoon psyllium husk powder

¼ teaspoon aluminum-free baking powder

1 pinch unrefined sea salt or Himalayan salt, or to taste

1 egg

1 tablespoon (15 ml) soda water (or any sparkling water)

Yield: 1 serving

1. Grease a microwave-safe cup with softened butter. (The higher and narrower the cup, the better the muffin will rise.)

2. Combine the almond flour, psyllium husk powder, baking powder, and salt in a small bowl, taking care to break up any lumps. Add the egg and mix well with a spoon. Add the carbonated water and mix well again. Spoon the batter into the greased cup, then microwave on high for 2 minutes. (Check the muffin after 1 minute and adjust the total cooking time according to your microwave oven.)

3. Remove the muffin from the cup, let cool slightly, slice, and enjoy warm with your favorite toppings, or toast it, if you like.

NUTRITION INFO
_____

IN TOTAL:
15.0 g protein;
22.3 g fat;
2.5 g net carbs;
270 kcal

SUGAR-FREE, STARCH-FREE PIE CRUST

Traditional pie crust is filled with starch—mainly wheat flour—which means it's hardly a healthy choice. Never fear, though: It's not difficult to make a thin, flaky starch-free pastry that's perfect for sweet and savory pies alike. If you're using this crust to make a sweet pie, add 2 tablespoons (16 g) of powdered erythritol to the dry ingredients, or a couple of drops liquid stevia to the wet ingredients.

INGREDIENTS

½ cup (60 g) almond flour

¼ cup (30 g) coconut flour

2 tablespoons (18 g) psyllium husk powder

1 teaspoon aluminum-free baking powder

Pinch unrefined sea salt or Himalayan salt

3 eggs

2 tablespoons (30 ml) light olive oil

Yield: 1 pie crust

1. Preheat the oven to 350ºF (175ºC). Place the dry ingredients in a small bowl and mix them well to break up any lumps.

2. Place the eggs and olive oil into a medium bowl. Gradually add the dry ingredients, whisking constantly to prevent lumps. (The dough will be very sturdy, and will thicken almost immediately after adding the dry ingredients.) Press the dough evenly into the bottom and sides of a 10-inch (25 cm) pie pan. Prick the dough all over with a fork to prevent blistering, and prebake the crust for 15 minutes before adding the filling of your choice.

NUTRITION INFO

IN TOTAL:

41.7 g protein;
79.0 g fat;
13.5 g net carbs;
932 kcal

PER SLICE,
IF 8 SLICES IN TOTAL:

5.2 g protein;
9.9 g fat;
1.7 g net carbs;
117 kcal

PER SLICE,
IF 12 SLICES IN TOTAL:

3.5 g protein;
6.6 g fat;
1.1 g net carbs;
78 kcal

VEGAN SUGAR-FREE, STARCH-FREE PIE CRUST

If you're vegan, you know that creating low-carb desserts can be a bit of an extra challenge. But here's some good news: You don't need egg to make a perfect pie crust. And this recipe is proof. Like its nonvegan counterpart (opposite page), it calls for just a few simple ingredients, and it can be used to make sweet and savory pies that are sure to impress your guests.

INGREDIENTS

2 cups (230 g) almond flour

2 tablespoons (18 g) psyllium husk powder

½ teaspoon unrefined sea salt or Himalayan salt, or to taste

1 teaspoon aluminum-free baking powder

⅓ cup (80 ml) extra-light olive oil

¼ cup (60 ml) water

Yield: 1 pie crust

Preheat the oven to 350°F (175°C). Place the almond flour, psyllium husk powder, salt, and baking powder in a small bowl. Mix well to break up any lumps. Add the olive oil and water. Use clean hands to mix and knead until a stiff dough forms. Press the dough evenly into the bottom and the sides of a 10-inch (25 cm) pie pan. Prick the dough all over with a fork to prevent blistering. Prebake the crust for 10 minutes before adding the filling of your choice.

NUTRITION INFO

IN TOTAL:
44.0 g protein;
174.2 g fat;
20.1 g net carbs;
1824 kcal

PER SLICE,
IF 8 SLICES IN TOTAL:

5.5 g protein;
21.8 g fat;
2.5 g net carbs;
228 kcal

PER SLICE,
IF 12 SLICES IN TOTAL:

3.7 g protein;
14.5 g fat;
1.7 g net carbs;
152 kcal

NUTRITION INFO

IN TOTAL:
8.5 g protein;
6.8 g fat;
1.0 g net carbs;
100 kcal

SINGLE-SERVE TORTILLA

Is there anything quite as handy and versatile as a tortilla? It can become a burrito, a quesadilla, or a lunchtime wrap—and when it's baked, it's the perfect foundation for a plate of nachos (see the variation, above right). And this starch-free version is a cinch to make. Because it has a neutral taste, it's perfect for desserts and sweet snacks, too.

INGREDIENTS

2 teaspoons coconut flour

1 teaspoon psyllium husk powder

Pinch unrefined sea salt or Himalayan salt

1 egg

2 teaspoons unsweetened almond milk

NOTE: For extra flavor and variety, add ½ teaspoon dried herbs or 1 teaspoon dried tomato powder to the dry ingredients.

VARIATION: To make nachos: Add 1 teaspoon extra-light olive oil to the batter and omit the almond milk. Bake the tortilla for 3 minutes, turning it over after each minute. Let cool completely. Once cooled, the tortilla will be crispy and easy to break into pieces.

Yield: 1 serving

1. Combine the coconut flour, psyllium husk powder, and salt in a small bowl and mix well until combined. Add the egg and the almond milk and stir with a spoon until smooth.

2. Pour the mixture onto an 8-inch (20 cm) microwave-safe plate. Tilt the plate to thinly spread the batter as evenly as possible. Heat on high for 1 minute and 45 seconds, or until done. Adjust the time according to your microwave oven, but don't overbake: The tortilla will be dry if baked too long. Use a spatula or cheese slicer to remove the tortilla from the plate. Let cool and serve.

TIP: You can use almond flour instead of coconut flour, if you like. Just omit the coconut flour and add 2 tablespoons (15 g) of almond flour to the dry ingredients and then follow the recipe directions.

SUPER-HEALTHY WAFFLES (OR PANCAKES)

While waffles are often thought of as breakfast food in the United States, in Europe they are eaten at every meal. You can top waffles with berries for breakfast, cream cheese and mixed greens for lunch, and hearty stews for a comforting dinner. With jam and whipped cream they are a very popular dessert. Waffles and pancakes make great substitutes to traditional high-carb options such as bread, croissants, and noodles; thus, they serve as a great basic recipe in your low-sugar cooking repertoire.

INGREDIENTS

½ cup (60 g) coconut flour

¼ cup (20 g) vanilla-flavored grass-fed whey protein

1 tablespoon (7 g) milled chia seeds

2 teaspoons aluminum-free baking powder

Pinch unrefined sea salt or Himalayan salt

6 eggs

½ cup (120 ml) unsweetened almond milk

20 drops vanilla stevia

TIP: For dairy-free waffles or pancakes, replace the whey protein with rice protein, and use butter-flavored coconut oil or light olive oil for frying.

Yield: 6 to 8 pancakes

1. Place the dry ingredients in a small bowl and mix well. Place the eggs, almond milk, and stevia in a medium bowl and whisk until smooth. Gradually add the dry ingredients to the wet, stirring constantly. When completely combined, let the mixture stand for 10 minutes to thicken.

2. Use the batter to make waffles in your waffle maker according to the manufacturer's instructions. (Use butter for greasing the waffle maker.) To make pancakes, fry pancakes in a small skillet on medium-low heat in an ample amount of butter. Store leftover pancakes or waffles in an airtight container in the fridge and consume within one day.

NUTRITION INFO

IN TOTAL:

72.0 g protein;
52.7 g fat;
17.3 g net carbs;
833 kcal

PER SERVING,
IF 6 SERVINGS IN TOTAL:

12.0 g protein;
8.8 g fat;
2.9 g net carbs;
139 kcal

PER SERVING,
IF 8 SERVINGS IN TOTAL:

9.0 g protein;
6.6 g fat;
2.2 g net carbs;
104 kcal

CHAPTER 5

BREAKFAST

When your body doesn't have to combat high insulin and blood sugar levels, you'll have lots more energy for your daily tasks. So why not start your day with a delicious, nutritious, sugar-free breakfast? The recipes in this chapter are designed to keep you satisfied for hours—until lunchtime, and then some. For a weekend brunch, pop the Five-Ingredient Overnight Sausage and Egg Breakfast Casserole on page 83 or the Puffy Cheese Omelet with Avocado on page 82 into the oven. Or on busy weekdays when you haven't got time to wait, the One-Minute Omelet in a Mug or Starch-Free Hot Cereal will satisfy you just in a few minutes.

For an even quicker option, bake some Hearty Breakfast Muffins with Bacon and Cheese on page 75 or Scrummy Streusel-Topped Blueberry Muffins on page 76 ahead of time, then take them as an easy grab-and-go breakfast. (Just be prepared for some jealous glances on your commute.) Ready to become a morning person?

LUSCIOUS KEY LIME PIE SMOOTHIE WITH A SECRET INGREDIENT

If you love Key lime pie, I've got great news for you: You can have it for breakfast. This healthy green smoothie is packed with good-for-you ingredients—and don't worry if you can't find Key limes. It's just as good when it's made with regular ones. And can you guess the secret ingredient? It's one of the all-time best superfoods: sprouts. (Just don't tell your kids!)

Yield: 1 serving

Simply place all ingredients in a high-speed blender and blend until smooth. If you use xanthan gum, be sure to sprinkle it on top of the mixture before blending to prevent lumping.

INGREDIENTS

1 cup (240 ml) unsweetened almond milk

½ cup (115 g) plain full-fat Greek or Turkish yogurt

⅓ cup (43 g) powdered erythritol

Zest of 1 small lime or zest of three Key limes

1½ tablespoons (22 ml) freshly squeezed lime juice

1 cup (50 g) well-rinsed and drained sprouts (broccoli, alfalfa, etc.), tightly packed

½ teaspoon glucomannan or xanthan gum, for thickening (optional)

VARIATION: Add 2 peeled and pitted ripe Hass avocados for a delicious Key Lime Pie Pudding! Divide the mixture between serving bowls and enjoy with a spoon.

NUTRITION INFO

IN TOTAL:
6.7 g protein;
14.8 g fat;
8.7 g net carbs;
209 kcal

NUTRITION INFO

IN TOTAL:
16.9 g protein;
54.4 g fat;
5.4 g net carbs;
587 kcal

JOYFUL CHOCOLATE ALMOND SMOOTHIE

This guilt-free smoothie won't spike your blood sugar levels like pastries or sugary candy bars will, making it a delicious, no-cheat start to the morning, and its carefully chosen ingredients will nourish and satisfy both body and mind. (Think of it as brain food!) Plus, this smoothie is vegan and dairy-free, which means it's the ideal start to your day if you don't tolerate dairy.

INGREDIENTS

1 cup (240 ml) unsweetened almond milk

¼ cup (60 g) unsweetened almond butter

2 tablespoons (15 g) unsweetened dark cocoa powder

1 tablespoon (14 g) extra-virgin coconut oil

3 tablespoons (24 g) powdered erythritol

1 teaspoon vanilla extract

Yield: 1 serving

Simply place all the ingredients in a high-speed blender and blend until smooth. Serve immediately.

NUTRITION INFO

CHOPPED WALNUTS USED
IN CALCULATIONS

IN TOTAL:
42.1 g protein;
166.2 g fat;
28.3 g net carbs;
1786 kcal

PER SERVING,
IF 4 SERVINGS IN TOTAL:
10.5 g protein;
41.5 g fat;
7.1 g net carbs;
446 kcal

INSTANT LEMON CHEESECAKE YOGURT PARFAITS

Baking lemon cheesecake takes hours, and worse, you have to wait until the next day to eat it. (Who has that kind of patience? Not me!) But these Lemon Cheesecake Yogurt Parfaits only take a minute or two to make. And their rich, sophisticated taste is absolutely decadent. So if you're craving something indulgent yet healthy and sating for breakfast, look no further than these quickie treats.

Yield: 4 servings

1. Place the yogurt, cream cheese, lemon juice, and lemon stevia into a small bowl. Mix well with a spoon until smooth. Adjust the taste by adding more cream cheese, lemon juice, or lemon stevia, if necessary. Mix well again.

2. Place ¼ cup (32 g) of the granola or chopped nuts into four serving glasses or small mason jars, and top each with one quarter of the yogurt mixture. Garnish each with ½ tablespoon (4 g) granola and serve immediately.

INGREDIENTS

2 cups (460 g) thick, plain full-fat Turkish or Greek yogurt

½ cup (120 g) plain full-fat cream cheese

1 tablespoon (15 ml) freshly squeezed lemon juice

100 drops lemon stevia, or to taste

1 cup (130 g) Grain-Free Granola, page 68, or chopped nuts of choice, plus 2 tablespoons (16 g) for garnish

TIP: Not a fan of cream cheese? No problem: This recipe works just as well as a lemon yogurt parfait, minus the cream cheese. Just use 2½ cups (600 ml) plain full fat yogurt and omit the cream cheese.

GRAIN-FREE GRANOLA

This healthy, grain-free granola is great for your gut, and you can think of this recipe as a template for endless variations: Use whichever nuts and seeds you happen to have on hand. And feel free to reduce the amount of erythritol if you don't like your granola very sweet—but don't replace it or omit it completely because it's the secret ingredient that makes this granola deliciously crunchy.

INGREDIENTS

½ cup (20 g) unsweetened coconut flakes

½ cup (45 g) almond flakes

½ cup (65 g) chopped pecans

½ cup (75 g) sunflower seeds

¼ cup (25 g) erythritol crystals

1 tablespoon (15 ml) melted extra-virgin coconut oil

1 teaspoon Ceylon cinnamon

½ teaspoon vanilla powder

Yield: about 2 cups (205 g)

1. Preheat the oven to 350ºF (175ºC). Line a baking sheet with parchment paper.

2. Place all the ingredients in a large bowl. Toss well to ensure everything is well mixed and the nuts, seeds, and coconut are covered with oil and seasonings. Transfer the mixture to the lined baking sheet, and spread it out evenly with a spoon into as thin a layer as possible.

3. Bake for 8 to 12 minutes, or until the mixture turns golden-brown. (Be careful, though, as the nuts can quickly become too dark and burn.) Remove the granola from the oven and let cool completely. The granola is soft and chewy while hot, but becomes crunchy when it has cooled down.

4. Break the cool granola into small pieces, and store in a tightly sealed glass jar in a cool, dry place.

TIP: Make Pumpkin Pie Spiced Grain-Free Granola. It's easy: Just replace the cinnamon with pumpkin pie spice.

NUTRITION INFO

IN TOTAL:
34.4 g protein;
132.9 g fat;
17.9 g net carbs;
1411 kcal

PER ¼ CUP (25 G):
4.3 g protein;
16.6 g fat;
2.2 g net carbs;
176 kcal

PER TABLESPOON (6 G):
1.1 g protein;
4.2 g fat;
0.6 g net carbs;
44 kcal

STARCH-FREE HOT CEREAL

If you're following a gluten-free, low-sugar diet, a traditional breakfast of porridge or oatmeal isn't an option. But this simple, healthy alternative is just as good—and it's packed with nutrients, too. Top it with berries, sugar-free syrup, or a sizeable pat of grass-fed butter, and you've got a warming, satisfying, low-carb breakfast that'll see you through even the darkest winter mornings.

NOTE: Mix things up a little: use unsweetened almond milk or heavy cream instead of water for a richer taste.

Yield: 1 serving

1. Combine all ingredients in a small saucepan, and place over a medium-low heat, stirring continuously and breaking the almond butter lumps into smaller pieces with the back of a spoon.

2. When the mixture is smooth, hot, and thick, remove the saucepan from the heat. Let cool slightly, and serve with fresh berries or a pat of grass-fed butter, if you like.

INGREDIENTS

⅓ cup (80 g) unsweetened almond butter

2 teaspoons milled chia seeds

⅓ cup (80 ml) water

1 pinch unrefined sea salt or Himalayan salt, or to taste

TIP: Almond butter suits this hot "cereal" especially well, but feel free to experiment with different nut butters.

NUTRITION INFO

IN TOTAL:
18.4 g protein;
46.3 g fat;
5.4 g net carbs;
511 kcal

LUSCIOUS LOW-SUGAR FRENCH TOAST

Just a quick glance at the ingredient list for classic French toast confirms that it's full of sugar and starch—a major no-no if you're following a low-sugar lifestyle. But my healthy version tastes just as good—even better!—and has practically no sugar at all. Be sure to use a sufficiently high heat for frying to keep your French toast from getting soggy.

INGREDIENTS

FOR THE FRENCH TOAST:

4 eggs

¼ cup (60 ml) unsweetened almond milk

1 teaspoon vanilla extract

1 teaspoon Ceylon cinnamon

5 drops liquid stevia

8 slices Easy Fluffy Bread (page 53)

Butter for frying

FOR TOPPING:

Freshly grated nutmeg (optional)

¼ cup (60 g) grass-fed butter

⅓ cup (80 ml) Homemade Sugar-Free Maple Syrup, page 52

Yield: 4 servings

1. Prepare the French toast. Place the eggs, almond milk, vanilla extract, cinnamon, and stevia in a medium bowl. Whisk well to combine. (If the cinnamon floats on top of the mixture, just continue to whisk until it has become well incorporated.) Then soak each bread slice in the egg mixture for 10 seconds.

2. Heat a griddle or skillet over medium-high heat. When hot, melt a pat of butter in the skillet. Fry the bread slices for 3 to 4 minutes on each side, or until golden brown. To serve, sprinkle each slice of French toast with freshly grated nutmeg, if you like, and top with a pat of butter and Homemade Sugar-Free Maple Syrup (page 52).

TIP: Making French toast for the holidays? Replace the almond milk with ⅓ cup (80 ml) Rich Sugar-Free Eggnog (page 183) or use Low-Sugar Cinnamon Raisin Bread (page 54) instead of Easy Fluffy Bread.

NOTE: Sprinkle shaved dark chocolate (with a minimum cocoa content of 85 percent) on the freshly fried bread slices. The chocolate melts and creates an incredibly chocolatey—but guilt-free!—treat.

NUTRITION INFO

IN TOTAL:

79.6 g protein;
176.2 g fat;
14.5 g net carbs;
1963 kcal

PER SERVING,
IF 4 SERVINGS IN TOTAL:

19.9 g protein;
44.0 g fat;
3.6 g net carbs;
491 kcal

NUTRITION INFO

IN TOTAL:

65.1 g protein;
87.8 g fat;
27.4 g net carbs;
1167 kcal

PER MUFFIN,
IF 10 MUFFINS IN TOTAL:

6.5 g protein;
8.8 g fat;
2.7 g net carbs;
117 kcal

SPLENDID SUN-DRIED TOMATO, BASIL, AND PINE NUT MUFFINS

Bursting with fresh flavors, these breakfast muffins are a wonderfully savory way to start your day. They're topped with piquant pine nuts, spotted with bold basil, and dotted with succulent sun-dried tomatoes. They're baked at a low oven temperature, so they're exceptionally moist. Make them ahead of time and freeze them. In the morning, all you need to do is pop a couple into the microwave, and you're good to go.

INGREDIENTS

½ cup (60 g) coconut flour

2 teaspoons aluminum-free baking powder

1 teaspoon onion powder

6 eggs

½ cup (20 g) finely chopped fresh basil leaves, loosely packed

⅓ cup (35 g) finely chopped sun-dried tomatoes

¼ cup (60 ml) heavy cream or coconut cream

½ teaspoon unrefined sea salt or Himalayan salt, or to taste

2 tablespoons (18 g) pine nuts

Yield: 10 muffins

1. Preheat the oven to 300ºF (150ºC). Line a muffin pan with paper liners.

2. Combine the coconut flour, baking powder, and onion powder in a small bowl. Mix well to break up any lumps.

3. Place the eggs, basil, tomatoes, cream, and salt in a medium bowl. Whisk well until combined. Gradually add the dry ingredients to the wet, whisking all the time to prevent lumping.

4. Scoop the batter into the muffin liners, filling them three-quarters full. Top each with a sprinkle of pine nuts, gently pressing the nuts into the muffin batter so that they stick. Bake for 20 to 30 minutes, or until a toothpick inserted in the middle of a muffin comes out almost dry. Don't overbake. Remove from the oven, let cool, and serve warm.

WHOLESOME CORN-FREE SPINACH AND ARTICHOKE "CORN" MUFFINS

Coarse almond flour, often sold as almond meal, is a perfect substitute for starchy cornmeal. The texture is similar, and the flavor is rich and nutty. What's more, almond flour contains lots of nutrients and few natural sugars—unlike corn flour, which is nutrient-poor. So it's an ideal ingredient in these savory breakfast muffins, which take their inspiration from classic spinach and artichoke dip.

Yield: 12 muffins

1. Preheat the oven to 350°F (175°C). Line a muffin pan with paper liners.

2. Combine all ingredients in a medium bowl. Mix well until a smooth batter is achieved. Scoop the batter into the muffin liners, filling them three-quarters full. Bake for 25 to 30 minutes, or until a toothpick inserted in the middle of a muffin comes out almost dry. Remove from the oven, let cool slightly, and serve warm. Freeze the leftovers.

INGREDIENTS

1½ cups (165 g) coarse almond flour

1 cup (90 g) shredded cheddar or Monterey Jack cheese

1 cup (50 g) finely chopped baby spinach, loosely packed

4 medium canned artichoke hearts, drained and chopped

3 eggs

¼ cup (60 ml) heavy cream

1 teaspoon unrefined sea salt or Himalayan salt, or to taste

NUTRITION INFO

IN TOTAL:
87.1 g protein;
153.7 g fat;
20.0 g net carbs;
1811 kcal

PER MUFFIN,
IF 12 MUFFINS IN TOTAL:
7.3 g protein;
12.8 g fat;
1.7 g net carbs;
151 kcal

HEARTY BREAKFAST MUFFINS WITH BACON AND CHEESE

These stick-to-your-ribs breakfast muffins are a dream come true for busy mornings. Prepare them beforehand and freeze. When hunger hits, just pop one in the microwave, then grab and go. Because they're sure to tide you over till dinner, they make a great take-along midafternoon snack for school or work, too. There's no need to stick to bacon and cheese here, either. You can create endless variations using different cheeses, meats, or veggies.

Yield: 8 to 12 muffins

1. Preheat the oven to 350°F (175°C). Line a muffin pan with paper liners.

2. Combine the coconut flour and the baking powder in a small bowl, then mix the rest of the ingredients in a large bowl until well mixed. Add the coconut flour mixture to the bowl with the rest of the ingredients and mix with a fork until the batter is smooth.

3. Scoop the batter into the muffin liners, filling them three-quarters full. Bake for 20 minutes, or until a toothpick inserted in the center of a muffin comes out almost dry. Remove from the oven, let cool slightly, and serve warm. Freeze the leftovers.

INGREDIENTS

¼ cup (30 g) coconut flour

1 teaspoon aluminum-free baking powder

1 teaspoon onion powder

1 teaspoon Cajun seasoning

5 eggs

¼ cup (60 ml) heavy cream

1½ cups (145 g) shredded Swiss cheese (or other sharp cheese)

1 cup (140 g) chopped raw bacon

½ teaspoon unrefined sea salt, or to taste

¼ cup (55 g) finely chopped pickled, drained jalapeños (optional)

NOTE: These muffins are really hearty and satisfying, so serve them with some raw veggies, such as carrots or celery sticks, for a well-balanced breakfast or snack.

NUTRITION INFO

IN TOTAL:
105.8 g protein;
138.6 g fat;
11.4 g net carbs;
1717 kcal

PER MUFFIN,
IF 8 MUFFINS IN TOTAL:
13.2 g protein;
17.3 g fat;
1.4 g net carbs;
215 kcal

PER MUFFIN,
IF 12 MUFFINS IN TOTAL:
8.8 g protein;
11.6 g fat;
1.0 g net carbs;
143 kcal

SCRUMMY STREUSEL-TOPPED BLUEBERRY MUFFINS

Topped with lip-licking streusel, sugar-free blueberry muffins have never tasted this good before! Here's why: This recipe uses a lower oven temperature to prevent the (starch-free) streusel from getting too dark, and to keep the muffins deliciously moist. Wild blueberries are the most nutritious—and the most natural—option, so go for them if you can find them.

INGREDIENTS

FOR THE STREUSEL:

¾ cup (90 g) chopped pecans

2 tablespoons (26 g) erythritol crystals

½ teaspoon Ceylon cinnamon

1½ tablespoons (25 ml) melted grass-fed butter or extra-virgin coconut oil

FOR THE MUFFINS:

4 eggs

⅓ cup (80 ml) heavy cream or coconut milk

⅓ cup (33 g) erythritol crystals

20 drops vanilla stevia, or to taste

½ cup (60 g) coconut flour

½ cup (75 g) frozen wild blueberries

Yield: 10 muffins

1. Preheat the oven to 300°F (150°C). Line a muffin pan with paper liners.

2. Prepare the streusel: Combine all the streusel ingredients in a medium bowl. Mix well with a spoon. Set aside.

3. Prepare the muffin batter: Place the eggs, cream, erythritol, and vanilla stevia in a medium bowl and mix well. Gradually add the coconut flour, mixing all the time to prevent lumping. Fold in the frozen blueberries. Scoop the batter into the muffin liners, filling them three-quarters full. Divide the streusel between the muffins, gently pressing it into the muffin batter so it sticks. Bake for 30 to 40 minutes, or until a toothpick inserted in the middle of a muffin comes out almost dry. Remove from the oven, let cool slightly, and serve, or freeze for 1 to 2 months.

NUTRITION INFO

WITH STREUSEL

IN TOTAL:

53.7 g protein;
145.8 g fat;
24.1 g net carbs;
1635 kcal

PER MUFFIN,
IF 10 MUFFINS IN TOTAL:

5.3 g protein;
14.6 g fat;
2.5 g net carbs;
164 kcal

WITHOUT STREUSEL

IN TOTAL:

44.5 g protein;
62.5 g fat;
19.6 g net carbs;
827 kcal

PER MUFFIN,
IF 10 MUFFINS IN TOTAL:

4.4 g protein;
6.3 g fat;
2.0 g net carbs;
83 kcal

TWO-MINUTE RASPBERRY CREAM CHEESE BREAKFAST IN A MUG

Cheesecake? Sweet omelet? Call this dish whatever you like. It's both tasty beyond belief and immensely satisfying. It features juicy raspberries in a rich cheesecake-like texture, and the egg adds a dose of satiating protein. Try it with other berries, too, and feel free to add spices to taste, such as cinnamon and ginger.

Yield: 1 serving

Combine all the ingredients in a small microwave-safe ramekin or mug. Mix well. Cook in the microwave oven on high for 1 minute and 30 seconds, or until the "omelet" is cooked around the edges but is still jiggling in the center. Don't over-bake. Let cool slightly and then serve with fresh berries and whipped cream.

INGREDIENTS

2 ounces (60 g) full-fat cream cheese

¼ cup (25 g) frozen raspberries

1 egg

10 drops vanilla stevia, or to taste

NUTRITION INFO

IN TOTAL:
11.4 g protein;
20.4 g fat;
3.1 g net carbs;
242 kcal

ONE-MINUTE OMELET IN A MUG

Consuming protein in the morning can really help boost your energy levels throughout the day, and that's where this sixty-second, mess-free breakfast comes in: All you need is a mug and a microwave. To turn it into a full breakfast, serve it with raw vegetables and some starch-free bread. You can also add chopped ham or salami to the egg and butter mixture before cooking.

INGREDIENTS

1 tablespoon (14 g) grass-fed butter

2 eggs

1 to 2 tablespoons (5 to 10 g) grated Parmesan cheese

Unrefined sea salt or Himalayan salt and freshly ground black pepper, to taste

Yield: 1 serving

Place the butter in a small microwave-safe ramekin or cup. Heat on high for 10 seconds, or until melted. Add the eggs to the ramekin or cup with the melted butter. Prick the yolks with a fork to prevent them from splattering in the microwave. Stir gently to mix the eggs and butter, then sprinkle the Parmesan on top. Place the ramekin or cup in the microwave, and cover with a microwave plate cover. Heat on high for 40 to 50 seconds, or until the omelet is just done but still creamy. (Adjust the time to suit your microwave oven.) Don't overbake: The omelet will turn out dry if baked too long. Season with salt and pepper and serve immediately.

NUTRITION INFO

IN TOTAL:
16.8 g protein;
25.4 g fat;
0.4 g net carbs;
298 kcal

NUTRITION INFO

IN TOTAL:

32.7 g protein;
36.2 g fat;
5.5 g net carbs;
480 kcal

PER SERVING,
IF 2 SERVINGS IN TOTAL:

16.3 g protein;
18.1 g fat;
2.8 g net carbs;
240 kcal

QUICK PIZZA OMELET

Wait a minute! Pizza for breakfast? That's right—and there's no need to feel guilty about this low-carb version. It's big on protein and healthy fats, and best of all, it's easy to change up: Just use different meats, cheeses, veggies, or whatever leftovers happen to be lurking in the fridge. This recipe makes a satisfying breakfast for one ravenous person—or two moderately hungry ones.

INGREDIENTS

2 tablespoons (28 ml) heavy cream

¼ teaspoon garlic powder

¼ teaspoon onion powder

Unrefined sea salt, to taste

2 eggs

1 tablespoon (14 g) grass-fed butter or extra-virgin coconut oil, for frying

2 tablespoons (31 g) unsweetened tomato sauce

3 slices ham or pepperoni (or more or less to taste)

5 black Kalamata olives, pitted and sliced

1½ ounces (45 g) shredded mozzarella cheese

¼ teaspoon dried oregano

Yield: 2 servings

1. Mix the cream, garlic powder, onion powder, and salt together until well-combined and free from lumps. Add the eggs and mix gently with a fork.

2. Heat a skillet over medium heat and melt the butter or coconut oil in it. Pour the egg mixture into the skillet and cook, carefully pushing the cooked parts at the edges toward the center with a spatula. When the omelet is done around the edges but still jelly-like at the center, top with the tomato sauce, ham or pepperoni, olives, cheese, and oregano. Cover and cook for 2 minutes more, or until the cheese is melted. Serve immediately.

PUFFY CHEESE OMELET WITH AVOCADO

Yield: 6 servings

The secret to an impressively puffy omelet is to bake it in the oven with a bowl filled with boiling water, to mimic a water bath. The result? A simple, filling breakfast that's perfect for weekends: Just pop the omelet into the oven, then chill out over coffee and the newspaper for half an hour or so until breakfast is ready.

1. Preheat the oven to 350°F (175°C). Grease a 1.5-quart (1.5 L) baking dish generously with softened butter.

2. Place the eggs, cheese, heavy cream, almond milk, and salt in a large bowl. Whisk until well mixed, then pour the mixture into the greased baking dish. Sprinkle the cheese evenly on top.

3. Place a small, shallow, ovenproof bowl on the lowest oven rack. Carefully fill the bowl three-quarters full with boiling water. Place the baking dish with the omelet mixture on the middle oven rack.

4. Bake for 30 to 40 minutes, or until the center is no longer wobbly. (Don't overbake, though, as the eggs will turn out too dry. If the surface starts to become too brown, cover the dish with aluminum foil.) Remove from the oven and let cool slightly. Serve warm, topped with avocado slices.

INGREDIENTS

Softened butter (for greasing the dish)

6 eggs

2 cups (155 g) shredded cheddar cheese or other sharp cheese

⅔ cup (160 ml) heavy cream

½ cup (120 ml) unsweetened almond milk

1 teaspoon unrefined sea salt or Himalayan salt, or to taste

2 ripe Hass avocados, peeled, pitted and sliced

TIP: You can add more fillings to the omelet, such as ham, sausage, cooked veggies, or bits and pieces of leftover cheese.

NUTRITION INFO

IN TOTAL:
93.6 g protein;
180.7 g fat;
7.4 g net carbs;
2049 kcal

PER SERVING,
IF 6 SERVINGS IN TOTAL:
15.6 g protein;
30.1 g fat;
1.2 g net carbs;
341 kcal

FIVE-INGREDIENT OVERNIGHT SAUSAGE AND EGG BREAKFAST CASSEROLE

Ripe tomatoes give this meaty, five-ingredient casserole a summery lift. Just be sure to choose firm ones: If your tomatoes are too ripe and soft, they might release too much liquid during baking. Patience is a virtue here, by the way. After removing the casserole from the oven, it's important to let it stand for 15 minutes before serving to keep the moisture from leaking out. It'll be worth the wait—I promise.

Yield: 6 servings

1. Fry the sausage until cooked through, crumbling it with a wooden fork while frying. Spread the cooked sausage evenly into a 2-quart (2 L) baking dish. Top with the diced tomatoes and sprinkle the cheese on top. Mix together the eggs, heavy cream, salt, and pepper in a medium bowl. Pour the mixture evenly over the casserole. Cover, and refrigerate overnight.

2. When you're ready to bake the casserole, preheat the oven to 350ºF (175ºC). When hot, bake the casserole for 30 to 40 minutes, or until the cheese is golden brown and bubbly. Remove from the oven, let stand for 15 minutes, and then serve.

INGREDIENTS

1 pound (450 g) spicy bulk sausage

2 small firm Roma tomatoes, diced

2 cups (250 g) shredded mozzarella cheese

6 eggs

½ cup (120 ml) heavy cream

Unrefined sea salt or Himalayan salt and freshly ground black pepper, to taste

VARIATION: For an even more satisfying variation, spread 2 cups (180 g) cubed starch-free bread evenly in the bottom of the baking dish before adding the other ingredients.

NUTRITION INFO

VALUES HIGHLY DEPEND ON THE USED INGREDIENTS

IN TOTAL:
178.4 g protein;
228.8 g fat;
18.3 g net carbs;
2836 kcal

PER SERVING,
IF 6 SERVINGS IN TOTAL:

29.7 g protein;
38.1 g fat;
3.1 g net carbs;
473 kcal

NUTRITION INFO

IN TOTAL:
25.8 g protein;
33.7 g fat;
4.8 g net carbs;
425 kcal

EASY BREAKFAST BURRITO

With some Single-Serve Tortillas (page 61) on hand, it's a snap to whip up this spicy, savory breakfast burrito—even on the busiest mornings. You can vary this burrito endlessly, too: Just use your favorite starch-free vegetables, meat or fish, and season with your choice of spices and seasonings. And it's a great way to use up the leftovers lingering in your fridge.

INGREDIENTS

¼ cup (20 g) chopped button mushrooms

¼ cup (40 g) chopped green bell pepper

2 eggs

2 tablespoons (28 ml) water

1 teaspoon unsweetened sambal oelek or chili paste, or to taste

½ teaspoon onion powder

¼ teaspoon unrefined sea salt or Himalayan salt, or to taste

Oil or butter for frying

1 Single-Serve Tortilla (page 61)

2 tablespoons (30 ml) Low-Sugar Sweet and Sour Sauce (page 38)

2 tablespoons (16 g) sliced black Kalamata olives

Yield: 1 serving

1. Place the mushrooms, bell pepper, eggs, water, sambal oelek, onion powder, and salt in a medium bowl. Stir well with a fork.

2. Heat a skillet over medium-low heat. Add the oil or butter. When hot, add the egg mixture and cook, stirring slowly all the time, until the eggs are scrambled but still creamy. (Don't overcook or the eggs will become dry.)

3. Place the Single-Serve Tortilla shell on a plate and spread with the Low-Sugar Sweet and Sour Sauce on one side. Add the scrambled eggs and then top with the sliced olives. Fold the other half of the tortilla over the filling and serve immediately.

QUICK CHORIZO AND CAULIFLOWER BREAKFAST HASH

There's no room for starchy potatoes in a low-sugar breakfast, but it's easy to replace them with tasty, healthy cauliflower, as in this full-bodied hash. You'll want to keep the cauliflower crunchy for the best texture and flavor here, so be sure you don't overcook it. Serve this simple but scrumptious dish with salsa or tomato relish, if you like, and add more nonstarchy vegetables for extra nutrients.

INGREDIENTS

Oil or butter for frying

1 large onion, chopped

2 garlic cloves, finely chopped

2 packages (10 ounces, or 280 g, each) frozen cauliflower florets

10 ounces (280 g) chorizo, chopped

4 eggs

Unrefined sea salt or Himalayan salt and freshly ground black pepper, to taste

Yield: 2 to 4 servings

1. Heat a skillet over medium-high heat. Add the oil or butter. When hot, add the onion and garlic. Cook until soft and translucent, about 5 minutes. Add the cauliflower and cook, mixing, until the cauliflower is hot. Don't overcook. Add the chorizo and cook, stirring, until the chorizo is slightly browned. Season with salt and pepper.

2. Fry the eggs in a separate skillet but keep the chorizo and cauliflower hash warm while doing so. Transfer the hash to serving plates and top each serving with a fried egg. Serve immediately.

NUTRITION INFO

IN TOTAL:

108.4 g protein; 122.2 g
fat; 29.1 g net carbs;
1639 kcal

PER SERVING,
IF 2 SERVINGS IN TOTAL:

54.2 g protein;
61.1 g fat;
14.5 g net carbs; 820
kcal

PER SERVING,
IF 4 SERVINGS IN TOTAL:

27.1 g protein;
30.6 g fat;
7.3 g net carbs;
410 kcal

FIFTEEN-MINUTE SPRING VEGETABLE AND FETA BREAKFAST HASH

Artichokes are to spring what butterflies are to summer, but preparing them from scratch is too much work for a busy morning. That's where canned artichoke hearts come in, offering all their characteristic sweetness and flavor. They shine alongside asparagus and radishes in this healthy vegetarian hash, which gets crowned with sliced avocado and tangy feta cheese.

INGREDIENTS

1 tablespoon (15 ml) extra-virgin olive oil

1 small zucchini (7 ounces, or 200 g), cubed

1 teaspoon onion powder

½ teaspoon garlic powder

14-ounce (400 g) can artichoke hearts, drained (large ones quartered; medium and small ones halved)

8 green asparagus spears, woody stems removed, and cut into 2-inch (5 cm) pieces

10 radishes, halved

½ teaspoon unrefined sea salt or Himalayan salt

4 ounces (115 g) feta cheese, crumbled

2 Hass avocados, peeled, pitted, and sliced

1 tablespoon (15 ml) freshly squeezed lemon juice

1 cup (20 g) chopped watercress

Yield: 2 servings

1. Add the oil to a skillet and place over medium-high heat. Add the zucchini, onion powder, and garlic powder. Cook, covered, until the zucchini is crisp-tender, about 5 minutes. Add the artichoke, asparagus, and radishes. Heat, stirring, until hot, but don't cook. Season with salt, and divide the hash between two serving plates. Sprinkle each with half the feta.

2. Arrange the sliced avocado on top of both servings, one avocado per serving. Drizzle the lemon juice on the avocado slices to prevent them from turning brown. Top both servings with watercress and serve immediately.

NOTE: Need more protein? Serve the breakfast hash with fried eggs.

NUTRITION INFO

IN TOTAL:
42.6 g protein;
87.1 g fat;
17.7 g net carbs;
1025 kcal

PER SERVING,
IF 2 SERVINGS IN TOTAL:
21.3 g protein;
43.5 g fat;
8.8 g net carbs;
512 kcal

CHAPTER 6

LUNCH

Whether you spend your day in the office or at home, having a satisfying lunch is a must in order to keep your energy levels up for the rest of the day. And if you're following a low-sugar lifestyle, you don't want to rely on your local burger joint or the sandwich bar down the street. Luckily, this chapter features plenty of low-sugar lunch recipes that are super portable as well as quick and easy to prepare, such as soups, salads, sandwiches, and wraps. In it, you'll find healthier versions of lots of your old favorites—Rich No-Potato Clam Chowder (page 94) and Pasta-Free Minestrone with Ham (page 96)—minus the starchy pasta and potatoes. And when you have a batch of Easy Fluffy Bread (page 53) and Single Serve Tortillas (page 61) on hand, it's easy to make lots of satisfying wraps and sandwiches, such as the Stellar Spinach Wrap on page 111, or the Effortless Egg Salad Sandwich on page 105. Hungry yet?

COMFORTING CHICKEN ZOODLE SOUP

Nourishing, homemade chicken noodle soup is the ultimate cure for just about any ailment. So, when lunchtime rolls around, grab a mug of this healthy, gluten-free, starch-free chicken zoodle soup, wrap yourself in a cozy blanket (unless you're at the office!), and let the healing begin.

INGREDIENTS

2 tablespoons (28 g) extra-virgin coconut oil

1 small onion, chopped

2 garlic cloves, minced

2 celery stalks, thinly sliced

½ teaspoon dried thyme

1 bay leaf

1½ quarts (1.4 L) chicken stock

6 black peppercorns

1½ ounces (45 g) carrot, cut into matchsticks

2 cups (440 g) shredded cooked chicken

Unrefined sea salt or Himalayan salt, to taste

7 ounces (200 g) zoodles (spiralized zucchini)

Finely chopped fresh parsley for garnish (optional)

TIP: If you don't have cooked chicken on hand, you can cook 22 ounces (625 g) of raw, diced chicken in a skillet until the juices run clear and then use it in this light soup.

Yield: 8 servings

1. Heat a large saucepan over medium heat and add the coconut oil, followed by the onion, garlic, celery, thyme, and bay leaf. Cook, stirring, for 5 minutes or until the onion is translucent. (Don't let it brown.) Add the chicken stock, peppercorns, and carrots and bring to a boil. Let simmer for 5 minutes.

2. Add the chicken and simmer until the chicken is heated through. Season with salt, add the zoodles, and stir well. (Don't continue to cook: The zoodles will easily turn mushy if cooked.) Serve immediately. Garnish each serving with fresh parsley, if you wish.

NUTRITION INFO

IN TOTAL:
136.4 g protein;
64.6 g fat;
6.7 g net carbs;
1153 kcal

PER SERVING,
IF 8 SERVINGS IN TOTAL:
17.0 g protein;
8.1 g fat;
0.8 g net carbs;
144 kcal

EASY BOUILLABAISSE

Bouillabaisse is a traditional French soup that features fish, seafood, and vegetables, as well as Provençal herbs. The fish used in classic bouillabaisse is usually bony, but feel free to use any type of fish you like—or even a number of different types, which adds dimension and variation. You can also replace the mussels with other seafood, or use canned mussels or clams if you can't find fresh ones.

INGREDIENTS

¼ cup (60 ml) extra-virgin olive oil

1 large onion, chopped

2 garlic cloves, crushed

14-ounce (400 g) can crushed or diced tomatoes

1 small fennel bulb, cut into strips

6 cups (1.4 L) fish stock

8 saffron threads

1 teaspoon dried thyme

1 tablespoon (6 g) freshly grated orange peel (orange part only), optional

1½ pounds (680 g) fish of your choice, cut into bite-size pieces

1 pound (450 g) shell-on mussels, scrubbed and debearded (dead mussels discarded)

2 teaspoons unrefined sea salt or Himalayan salt, or to taste

½ cup (30 g) chopped flat leaf parsley, loosely packed

NOTE: To serve the soup in the traditional way, serve the bouillon first alongside starch-free bread, such as Easy Fluffy Bread (page 53). Serve the fish on a separate plate after the bouillon.

Yield: 6 to 8 servings

1. Heat a large saucepan over medium-high heat. Add the olive oil, onion, and garlic. Cook, stirring, until translucent, about 5 minutes.

2. Add the tomatoes and bring to a boil. Then add the fennel, fish stock, saffron, thyme, and orange peel, if using. Lower the heat and simmer until the fennel is crisp-tender, about 10 to 15 minutes.

3. Add the fish and the mussels. Simmer, covered, until the fish flakes, and the mussels open, about 5 to 10 minutes. Discard any unopened mussels. Season with salt and garnish with parsley.

NUTRITION INFO

IN TOTAL:
22.0 g protein;
87.4 g fat;
33.9 g net carbs;
1014 kcal

PER SERVING,
IF 4 SERVINGS IN TOTAL:
5.5 g protein;
21.9 g fat;
8.5 g net carbs;
253 kcal

FIFTEEN-MINUTE THAI-INSPIRED PUMPKIN SOUP

Spicy, warming, and hearty, this five-ingredient soup is ready in no time. Prepare it in the morning and store a serving in an insulated food jar until lunchtime (the flavors improve when they have time to mingle for a couple of hours). For a little variation, try experimenting with different types of curry paste: Red, green, and yellow curry pastes all work well here. Top with a dollop of sour cream and a small handful of crumbled bacon for extra flavor and satiety.

Yield: 4 servings

Combine the pumpkin, curry paste, onion powder, salt, and heavy cream in a large saucepan. Mix until smooth. If necessary, add a little water for a thinner consistency. Heat over medium-high heat, stirring constantly. When the mixture starts to boil, reduce the heat to a minimum. Let it simmer for 5 to 10 minutes, until thoroughly hot. Serve with gluten-free low-sugar bread or crackers.

INGREDIENTS

2 cans (15 ounces, or 425 g, each) 100 percent pure pumpkin puree

1 to 2 tablespoons (15 to 30 g) Thai red curry paste

1 teaspoon onion powder

1 teaspoon unrefined sea salt or Himalayan salt, or to taste

1 cup (240 ml) heavy cream

Water, if necessary

RICH NO-POTATO CLAM CHOWDER

There's no need to use starchy potatoes to make the perfect clam chowder. Here, super-healthy cauliflower replaces tasteless, carb-laden potatoes, and there are no starchy thickeners, either; pureed cauliflower does the trick instead, while heavy cream adds richness and extra body. If you don't have clam juice, don't skip it or replace it with water. Use fish stock or bouillon instead.

INGREDIENTS

6 cups (670 g) cauliflower chopped into ½-inch (1.3 cm) chunks, divided

8 slices raw bacon

1 cup (170 g) diced carrots

¾ cup (100 g) finely chopped onion

¾ cup (120 g) diced celery

2 cans (6.5 ounces, or 184 g, each) minced clams

6.5-ounce (184 g) can chopped clams

2 cups (480 ml) heavy cream

2 cups (480 ml) clam juice

1 teaspoon unrefined sea salt or Himalayan salt, or to taste

Freshly ground white pepper

1 tablespoon (15 ml) fresh lemon juice (optional)

Yield: 8 servings

1. Cook 3 cups (335 g) of the chopped cauliflower until soft and tender. Carefully discard the water. In a blender, process the cauliflower into a smooth puree. Set aside.

2. Fry the bacon until crisp. Reserve the fat and set the bacon aside. Fry the carrots, onion, celery, and the remaining cauliflower in the bacon fat until slightly soft, about 5 minutes.

3. Meanwhile, drain the juice from the clams into a large saucepan. Add the heavy cream and the pureed cauliflower. Mix well and bring to a boil.

4. Add the cooked vegetables with the bacon fat to the saucepan and cook until tender, about 10 to 15 minutes. Add the clams and remove from the heat. (Don't cook the clams: they'll become tough.) Season with salt and pepper. Add 1 tablespoon (15 ml) fresh lemon juice if you prefer a slightly tangy flavor. Serve immediately, crumbling some of the bacon on top of each serving.

TIP: When choosing canned clams, be sure to select a version that's additive-free. Most canned clams contain sodium tripolyphosphate, which helps retain the clams' natural juices, and calcium disodium EDTA, to maintain color. So try to find a product that consists only of clams, salt, and water, but if you can't, choose whole clams and chop half of them into tiny pieces and half of them into larger chunks.

NUTRITION INFO

IN TOTAL:
129.5 g protein;
218.7 g fat;
60.4 g net carbs;
2764 kcal

PER SERVING,
IF 8 SERVINGS IN TOTAL:
16.2 g protein;
27.3 g fat;
7.6 g net carbs;
345 kcal

PASTA-FREE MINESTRONE WITH HAM

Minestrone is back! This "healthified" version of the classic Italian soup won't spike your blood sugar levels, and it won't stress out your gut. Instead, it'll pamper it with plenty of fiber and healthy fats. This soup isn't technically pasta-free, since it includes low-carb shirataki noodles, but it *is* free from the starchy noodles essential to the traditional version.

INGREDIENTS

2 tablespoons (28 ml) extra-virgin olive oil

1 large onion, chopped

2 garlic cloves, crushed

1 cup (105 g) sliced celery stalks

½ cup (80 g) diced carrot

4 cups (950 ml) chicken or vegetable stock

14-ounce (400 g) can crushed or diced tomatoes

1 cup (120 g) frozen green beans

2 packages (7 ounces, or 200 g, each) shirataki fettucine or tagliatelle, cooked and cut into 2-inch (5 cm) pieces

1½ cups (205 g) chopped ham

1 teaspoon unrefined sea salt or Himalayan salt, or to taste

¼ cup (10 g) chopped fresh basil leaves

Freshly grated Parmesan cheese, for serving (optional)

Yield: 6 servings

Heat a large saucepan over medium heat. Add the olive oil, onion, garlic, celery, and carrot. Cook until the onion is translucent, about 5 minutes. Add the stock and the crushed tomatoes and bring to a boil. Then add the green beans, shirataki, and ham. Reduce the heat to medium-low. Let simmer, covered, until the vegetables are tender, about 20 minutes. Season with salt. Serve with a sprinkling of chopped fresh basil and some grated Parmesan, if desired.

NUTRITION INFO

WITHOUT PARMESAN

IN TOTAL:
45.9 g protein;
37.4 g fat;
32.9 g net carbs;
650 kcal

PER SERVING,
IF 6 SERVINGS IN TOTAL:
7.7 g protein;
6.2 g fat;
5.5 g net carbs;
108 kcal

CHEF'S SALAD WITH BACON

Chock-full of protein and good-for-you fats, this classic salad is a true hunger-slayer. Just be sure to cook your bacon over low heat: This prevents nitrosamines—dangerous carcinogenic agents—from forming. (Believe it or not, the healthiest way to fry bacon is in the microwave.) Or, if you want to avoid nitrates completely, choose salted pork belly instead of bacon.

INGREDIENTS

FOR THE DRESSING:

¼ cup (60 g) full-fat sour cream

½ teaspoon raw apple cider vinegar

¼ teaspoon Cajun seasoning, or to taste

Pinch unrefined sea salt or Himalayan salt

1 drop liquid stevia (optional)

FOR THE SALAD:

2 cups (65 g) mixed salad greens

1 small tomato, cut into wedges

3-inch (7.5 cm) piece English cucumber, thinly sliced

1 ounce (30 g) cheddar cheese, cut into matchsticks

1 to 2 hard-boiled eggs, cut into wedges

2 slices cooked bacon, crumbled

Yield: 1 serving

1. First, prepare the dressing. Simply place all ingredients into a small bowl. Mix well and set aside.

2. Prepare the salad. Arrange the salad ingredients on a serving plate. Top with the dressing and serve immediately.

NOTE: You can also pack this salad for lunch on the go. Just pack the salad, bacon, and dressing in separate containers. When you're ready to eat, sprinkle the bacon on the salad and top with the dressing. Bon appétit!

NUTRITION INFO

IN TOTAL:
22.3 g protein;
44.8 g fat;
5.4 g net carbs;
515 kcal

NUTRITION INFO

IN TOTAL:
22.7 g protein;
79.4 g fat;
4.1 g net carbs;
832 kcal

PER SERVING,
IF 2 SERVINGS IN TOTAL:
11.3 g protein;
39.7 g fat;
2.1 g net carbs;
416 kcal

FIVE-INGREDIENT AVOCADO, BLEU CHEESE, AND PECAN SALAD

Ridiculously low in sugar but packed with full-on flavors, this simple salad is rich in healthy fats, thanks to the avocado and pecans. And both are a great match for rich, creamy bleu cheese, which adds a dose of decadence to the mix. Dress this salad with Quick Raspberry Vinaigrette (page 43) and serve it as a light lunch, or add cooked, cubed chicken or shrimp for a more satiating meal.

Yield: 2 servings

Arrange all the ingredients on a serving plate (or in a mason jar, for a portable version). Store in the fridge until ready to serve. Serve with Quick Raspberry Vinaigrette (page 43), or your favorite tangy salad dressing.

INGREDIENTS

2 cups (65 g) mixed salad greens, loosely packed

2 cups (60 g) fresh spinach leaves, loosely packed

1 medium Hass avocado, peeled, pitted, and cubed

¼ cup (60 g) crumbled unpasteurized bleu cheese

⅓ cup (60 g) chopped toasted pecans

NUTRITION INFO

WITH FANTASTIC FRENCH DRESSING

IN TOTAL:

61.2 g protein;
104.9 g fat;
35.3 g net carbs;
1340 kcal

PER SERVING,
IF 4 SERVINGS IN TOTAL:

15.3 g protein;
26.2 g fat;
8.8 g net carbs;
335 kcal

WITHOUT FANTASTIC FRENCH DRESSING

IN TOTAL:

60.9 g protein;
56.5 g fat;
34.8 g net carbs;
901 kcal

PER SERVING,
IF 4 SERVINGS IN TOTAL:

15.2 g protein;
14.1 g fat;
8.7 g net carbs;
225 kcal

GREEK SALAD WITH CHICKEN AND STRAWBERRIES

The perfect lunch for a sunny summer's day, this classic Greek salad gets freshened up with a scattering of juicy strawberries. But it's still plenty filling, thanks to the cooked chicken and tangy feta cheese. If you're taking it with you for lunch—on a picnic, perhaps?—be sure to store the salad and the dressing in separate containers to keep the salad from wilting.

Yield: 4 servings

Arrange the ingredients on four serving plates in the given order. Serve immediately with Fantastic French Dressing.

NOTE: Feeling fruity? For a merrier, berrier version of this salad, serve it with the Quick Raspberry Vinaigrette on page 43.

INGREDIENTS

FOR THE SALAD:

1 head iceberg lettuce, cut into thin strips

1 small red onion, thinly sliced

½ English cucumber, thinly sliced

4 small tomatoes, cut into wedges

16 black Kalamata olives

4 ounces (115 g) feta cheese, cubed

4 ounces (115 g) cooked chicken, cubed

7 ounces (200 g) fresh strawberries, cut into wedges

OTHER INGREDIENTS:

¼ cup (60 ml) Fantastic French Dressing (page 42), to serve

TIP: Make this a classic Greek salad by omitting the chicken, increasing the amount of feta to 7 ounces (200 g), and omitting the strawberries (although the strawberries do add a fresh, summery, succulent taste).

BOLD BEEF SALAD

Red meat often gets a bad rap. But the truth is that unprocessed red meat contains an ample amount of vitamins and nutrients, and can be part of a healthy diet when consumed in moderation. Try to buy grass-fed beef, if you can: It's more natural, and therefore healthier. And it's delicious in this salad, which, true to its name, is full of bold colors and flavors.

INGREDIENTS

1 tablespoon (15 ml) extra-virgin olive oil

4 ounces (115 g) beef sirloin, cut into bite-size strips

½ teaspoon unrefined sea salt or Himalayan salt, or to taste

Pinch freshly ground black pepper

½ red bell pepper, chopped

½ teaspoon onion powder

3 cups (100 g) mixed salad greens

1 cup (50 g) chopped Belgian endive

¼ cup (20 g) tightly packed arugula leaves (optional)

¼ cup (30 g) chopped pecans

Yield: 1 serving

1. Prepare the beef for the salad. Heat a skillet over high heat. Add the olive oil and the beef and cook until medium-well done. Season with salt and pepper. Remove the meat from the skillet and set aside.

2. Reduce the heat to medium. Add the bell pepper and the onion powder. Mix well and cook until the bell pepper is crisp-tender. Season with salt and pepper. Combine the beef and the bell pepper mixture and set aside to cool. (Reserve the grease from the pan and use it for other purposes, or add it to the salad dressing for extra flavor and healthy fats.)

3. Prepare the salad. Arrange the salad greens and the endive (and the arugula, if using) on a serving plate. Top with the beef and bell pepper mixture. Top the salad with the pecans. Serve immediately with a low-sugar dressing, such as Fantastic French Dressing (page 42) or Quick Raspberry Vinaigrette (page 43).

NUTRITION INFO

IN TOTAL:
27.6 g protein;
43.3 g fat;
4.3 g net carbs;
522 kcal

THE ULTIMATE MASON JAR SALAD

Mason jar salads are the ultimate lunch: They're healthy, versatile, satisfying, and are so easy to grab when you're on your way out the door. But you need to choose the right ingredients, and it's important to add them to the jar in the right order so that your crisp salad doesn't turn into a soggy mess. This is my favorite version—a complete meal of protein, good fats, and veggies.

Yield: 2 servings

Fill a wide-mouthed 1-quart (946 ml) mason jar with the ingredients in the given order. (Don't cheat! Adding the ingredients in this order helps prevent the salad from becoming soggy.) Close the lid tightly and store refrigerated until serving time.

NOTE: Be sure to use a wide-mouthed mason jar for easy fill-up.

INGREDIENTS

¼ cup (60 ml) Quick Raspberry Vinaigrette (page 43)

1 cup (120 g) chopped raw cauliflower

2-inch (5 cm) piece cucumber, cubed

1 ripe Hass avocado, peeled, pitted, and cubed

½ cup (90 g) cubed, cooked chicken

½ cup (115 g) cottage cheese or shredded mozzarella cheese

1 cup (35 g) mixed salad greens or torn lettuce leaves

3 tablespoons (90 g) chopped walnuts

NUTRITION INFO

IN TOTAL:
39.8 g protein;
96.2 g fat;
6.8 g net carbs;
1062 kcal

PER SERVING,
IF 2 SERVINGS IN TOTAL:
19.9 g protein;
48.1 g fat;
3.4 g net carbs;
531 kcal

EFFORTLESS EGG SALAD SANDWICH

Great for kids and grownups alike, this easy-to-make egg salad is a lunchtime crowd-pleaser. Make it a day or two in advance so that you'll have it on hand for an instant lunchbox filler. Then use it to make sandwiches with slices of Easy Fluffy Bread (page 53), wrap, and you're good to go. Add some raw veggies for a well-rounded meal. Carrot and celery sticks provide a nice crunch.

INGREDIENTS

FOR EGG SALAD:

8 eggs

½ cup (113 g) Foolproof One-Minute Mayo (page 41)

1 teaspoon dry mustard (that is, mustard powder or ground mustard seeds)

3 tablespoons (9 g) chopped chives

½ teaspoon unrefined sea salt or Himalayan salt, or to taste

OTHER INGREDIENTS:

8 slices Easy Fluffy Bread (page 53)

Yield: 4 servings

1. First, prepare the egg salad. Place the eggs in a large saucepan and cover with cold water. Cover with a lid. Bring the water to a boil, but remove the saucepan from the heat immediately when boiling starts. Let the eggs stand covered in hot water for 10 to 12 minutes.

2. Remove the eggs from the hot water and let cool completely in cold water. When the eggs are cool, peel them, place them on a large, shallow plate, and mash with a fork. Add the mayonnaise, mustard, and chives and stir until well mixed. Season with salt.

3. Divide the egg salad among 4 slices of bread. Spread the mixture evenly. Top each with one of the remaining bread slices to make sandwiches. Wrap the sandwiches in wax paper or plastic wrap and keep refrigerated until serving time.

TIP: To make curried egg salad, just replace the chives with 1 teaspoon of curry powder.

NUTRITION INFO

IN TOTAL:

106.2 g protein;
184.9 g fat;
13.4 g net carbs;
2143 kcal

PER SANDWICH,
IF 4 SANDWICHES IN TOTAL:

26.6 g protein;
46.2 g fat;
3.3 g net carbs;
536 kcal

QUICK TUNA SATAY SANDWICH

In Thailand, a typical satay meal consists of bread, meat, satay sauce, and cucumber onion relish. And these sandwiches contain all of the above—except they're made with starch-free Easy Fluffy Bread (page 53), so they're far healthier, but just as tasty. Oh, and a word of caution: Be sure to drain the tuna well, since the salad might separate if any water is left.

Yield: 4 servings

1. First, prepare the tuna satay salad. Place all the ingredients in a small bowl. Mix well and set aside.

2. Prepare the sandwiches. Place four slices of Easy Fluffy Bread on a plate. Divide the cucumber slices, then the onion slices evenly between the bread slices. Top each with equal portions of the tuna satay salad, then top each with the remaining slices of bread. Wrap the sandwiches in wax paper or plastic wrap and keep refrigerated until serving time.

INGREDIENTS

FOR TUNA SATAY SALAD:

6.5-ounce (185 g) can albacore tuna in water, drained

½ cup (120 ml) Simple and Succulent Satay Sauce (page 45)

2 teaspoons raw apple cider vinegar

Pinch cayenne pepper

¼ cup chopped fresh cilantro (optional)

OTHER INGREDIENTS:

8 slices Easy Fluffy Bread (page 53)

2-inch (5 cm) piece English cucumber, thinly sliced

1 small onion, thinly sliced

TIP: To make chicken satay sandwiches, just replace the tuna with shredded chicken.

NUTRITION INFO

IN TOTAL:
100.5 g protein;
95.2 g fat;
25.9 g net carbs;
1363 kcal

PER SANDWICH,
IF 4 SANDWICHES IN TOTAL:
25.1 g protein;
23.8 g fat;
6.5 g net carbs;
341 kcal

IRRESISTIBLE CURRIED VEGETABLE WRAP

Could this be the most delicious veggie wrap in the world? Possibly. It's filled with low-starch vegetables cooked quickly in a creamy coconut sauce, plus alfalfa sprouts for extra crunch, bulk, and nutrition. Feel free to prepare the vegetable sauce alone and serve it alongside a handful of starch-free crackers for a warm, spoonable lunch or dinner.

INGREDIENTS

½ cup (120 ml) coconut milk

2 teaspoons Thai green curry paste, or to taste

½ teaspoon onion powder

½ cup (60 g) grated zucchini

¼ cup (25 g) chopped leek

¼ cup (25 g) grated carrot

Unrefined sea salt or Himalayan salt, or to taste

4 Single-Serve Tortillas (page 61)

1 cup (20 g) alfalfa sprouts

Yield: 4 servings

1. Heat a skillet over high heat. Add the coconut milk, curry paste, and onion powder. Cook, stirring, for 1 minute until hot and smooth. Add the zucchini, leek, and carrot and cook, stirring often until the vegetables are crisp-tender and the coconut milk is reduced to a thick sauce. Season with salt.

2. Divide the vegetable mixture between the tortillas, spreading it into a thin, even layer. Repeat with the alfalfa sprouts. Roll into wraps, slice each in half, and serve.

NUTRITION INFO

IN TOTAL:
39.8 g protein;
49.2 g fat;
12.1 g net carbs;
650 kcal

PER SERVING,
IF 4 SERVINGS IN TOTAL:

9.9 g protein;
12.3 g fat;
3.0 g net carbs;
163 kcal

TERRIFIC TERIYAKI PORK SANDWICH

This Asian-inflected teriyaki pork salad sandwich is bursting with flavors and textures, thanks to a hit of fresh ginger, homemade teriyaki sauce, and crunchy sesame seeds. Then it's mellowed out with a dollop of mayonnaise, and the result is nothing short of delicious. And it's a great way to use up last night's leftover cooked pork, too.

Yield: 4 servings

1. First, prepare the teriyaki pork salad. Place all the ingredients in a small bowl. Mix well and set aside.

2. Prepare the sandwiches. Place four slices of Easy Fluffy Bread on a plate and divide the lettuce leaves between the bread slices. Top with a generous layer of teriyaki pork salad and spread evenly. Top each with the remaining slices of bread. Wrap the sandwiches in wax paper or plastic wrap and keep refrigerated until serving time.

INGREDIENTS

FOR TERIYAKI PORK SALAD:

½ cup (115 g) shredded cooked pork (preferably neck) or pulled pork

⅓ cup (80 g) Foolproof One-Minute Mayo (page 41)

3 tablespoons (18 g) finely chopped green onion

2 tablespoons (28 ml) No-Sugar Teriyaki Sauce (page 40)

1 tablespoon (8 g) whole sesame seeds

1 teaspoon freshly grated ginger

OTHER INGREDIENTS:

8 slices Easy Fluffy Bread (page 53)

4 lettuce leaves

VARIATION: Use the leftover teriyaki pork salad for making lettuce wraps: Spread the salad onto lettuce leaves, and then roll up into wraps for an easy, starch-free variation.

NUTRITION INFO

IN TOTAL:
75.7 g protein;
143.6 g fat;
15.1 g net carbs;
1664 kcal

PER SANDWICH,
IF 4 SANDWICHES IN TOTAL:
18.9 g protein;
35.9 g fat;
3.8 g net carbs;
416 kcal

NUTRITION INFO

IN TOTAL:

46.0 g protein;
65.1 g fat;
8.0 g net carbs;
803 kcal

PER SERVING,
IF 4 SERVINGS IN TOTAL:

11.5 g protein;
16.3 g fat;
2.0 g net carbs;
201 kcal

STELLAR SPINACH AND CREAM CHEESE WRAP

This super-nutritious vegetarian lunch is a great way to sneak extra green veggies into your diet. These wraps are amazingly fresh and crispy, thanks to the spinach and sesame seeds, and a good *schmear* of full-fat cream cheese means they're sating, too. And they're a great canvas for your favorite seasonings, so go ahead and dress them up with, say, chili powder, Cajun seasoning, or curry powder before rolling them up and digging in.

Yield: 4 servings

Place each Single-Serve Tortilla on a plate and spread with 1 ounce (30 g) cream cheese. Top each with 1 teaspoon sesame seeds and season with salt and pepper. Then spread ½ cup (15 g) of the spinach leaves on each tortilla, roll them up into wraps, slice each in half, and serve.

INGREDIENTS

4 Single-Serve Tortillas (page 61)

4 ounces (115 g) full-fat cream cheese

4 teaspoons (11 g) whole sesame seeds

Unrefined sea salt or Himalayan salt and freshly ground black pepper, to taste

2 cups (60 g) fresh spinach leaves

VARIATION: For heartier wraps, add 2 ounces (60 g) lox. Divide it among the tortillas just before rolling them up into wraps.

COZY CHEESEBURGER WRAP

Who doesn't love a juicy cheeseburger? The traditional versions, unfortunately, are far from healthy, not least because of their starchy buns. But these low-carb cheeseburger wraps—which include all the trimmings—are comfort food at its best. Treat yourself to them for a special at-home lunch, or whip up a whole batch for dinner, and let family members make their own wraps at the table.

Yield: 4 servings

Fry the ground beef in oil or butter until cooked through and crumbly. Season with the onion powder, garlic powder, salt, and pepper. Spread each tortilla with 1 tablespoon (14 g) of mayonnaise, then top each with a quarter of the meat, tomatoes, and cheese. Roll each tortilla carefully into a wrap, slice in half, and serve immediately.

INGREDIENTS

6 ounces (170 g) ground beef

Oil or butter for frying

½ teaspoon onion powder

¼ teaspoon garlic powder

Unrefined sea salt or Himalayan salt and freshly ground black pepper, to taste

4 Single-Serve Tortillas (page 61)

¼ cup (56 g) Foolproof One-Minute Mayo (page 41)

¼ cup (50 g) finely diced tomatoes

1 cup (135 g) grated cheddar cheese

NUTRITION INFO

IN TOTAL:
102.1 g protein;
133.7 g fat;
5.0 g net carbs;
1632 kcal

PER SERVING,
IF 4 SERVINGS IN TOTAL:
25.5 g protein;
33.4 g fat;
1.2 g net carbs;
408 kcal

NUTRITIOUS BRIE, ORANGE, AND WALNUT WRAP

To whip up this sweet-and-savory (yet low-sugar!) vegetarian wrap, all you need are a few pantry basics—such as the Low-Sugar Orange Marmalade on page 48, and a Single-Serve Tortilla. After that, it's a cinch. It makes a filling after-work or after-school snack, too—and that's a lifesaver when you're just too hungry to hang on until dinner. Or, turn it into a complete meal by adding raw vegetables or a fresh green salad on the side.

INGREDIENTS

3 tablespoons (45 g) Low-Sugar Orange Marmalade (page 48)

1 Single-Serve Tortilla (page 61)

2 ounces (60 g) Brie cheese, sliced

2 tablespoons (15 g) chopped walnuts

TIP: Try other soft-ripened white cheeses, such as Camembert, in place of the Brie.

Yield: 1 serving

Spread the Low-Sugar Orange Marmalade evenly over the tortilla. Top with the Brie and sprinkle the chopped walnuts on top. Roll into a tight wrap, then slice in half and serve, or wrap in parchment paper and pack for lunch.

FIVE-INGREDIENT
BLT LETTUCE WRAP

It's always a good idea to keep some cooked bacon in the fridge for a low-carb snack—or for quickie lunches such as this one. Here, the classic BLT gets a makeover as a trendy, healthy lettuce wrap (no starchy white bread in sight!). Because it features just a few simple ingredients, it's ideal for busy mornings when you only have a few minutes to pull a packed lunch together.

Yield: 4 servings

Place the bacon, mayo, cheese, and cherry tomatoes into a small bowl. Mix well. Divide the mixture between the lettuce leaves and spread evenly. Roll into wraps and serve.

INGREDIENTS

8 slices fried bacon, crumbled

¼ cup (56 g) Foolproof One-Minute Mayo (page 41)

¼ cup (30 g) shredded cheddar cheese

8 cherry tomatoes, finely diced

4 large leaves romaine lettuce

NUTRITION INFO

IN TOTAL:

29.1 g protein;
97.6 g fat;
2.2 g net carbs;
1005 kcal

PER WRAP,
IF 4 WRAPS IN TOTAL:

7.3 g protein;
24.4 g fat;
0.5 g net carbs;
251 kcal

CHAPTER 7

DINNER

If you're coming home from work tired and hungry, spending hours in the kitchen isn't going to be on the agenda. You need a family-friendly meal that's quick, healthy, and satisfying. And the low-sugar recipes in this chapter have you covered; whether you're cooking for one person or the whole gang, you'll find plenty of options in the pages that follow. Pies and tarts, for instance, such as the Five-Ingredient Salmon Dill Quiche on page 117 or the Savory Ricotta Butternut Squash Tart (my new family favorite!) are simple to prepare, but make filling, elegant dinners. You might be surprised to learn that you can make sugar-free versions of some of your old standbys—for example, the Better than Macaroni and Cheese on page 126, or the Fuss-Free, Starch-Free Lasagna on page 122. If you're cooking for just yourself, try single-serving wonders such as my Skinny Tuna Pasta with Shirataki Noodles on page 131, or the Quick Chicken Fajita Pasta on page 132; both are easy, light options. Which will you make tonight?

NUTRITION INFO

WITHOUT CRUST

IN TOTAL:

123.7 g protein;
156.6 g fat;
7.9 g net carbs;
1936 kcal

PER SLICE,
IF 8 SLICES IN TOTAL:

15.5 g protein;
19.6 g fat;
1.0 g net carbs;
242 kcal

PER SLICE,
IF 12 SLICES IN TOTAL:

10.3 g protein;
13.1 g fat;
0.7 g net carbs;
161 kcal

FIVE-INGREDIENT SALMON DILL QUICHE

It's easy to make a scrumptious, healthy quiche for tonight's dinner: All you need is five basic ingredients. And the result is a hot, flavorful meal that's bursting with fresh herbs and healthy fats. This quiche is crust-free, but if you'd like to include one, just prepare a batch of Vegan Sugar-Free, Starch-Free Pie Crust (page 59) and prebake it for fifteen minutes before adding the filling.

Yield: 8 to 12 servings

Preheat the oven to 350°F (175°C). Combine the salmon, heavy cream, eggs, and dill in a large bowl. Season with salt. Whisk well and then pour the mixture into a 10-inch (25 cm) pie pan. Spread the shredded cheese evenly on top and bake in the preheated oven for 25 minutes, or until the cheese is melted, golden brown, and bubbly. Remove from the oven, let set 5 minutes, and serve. Store leftovers in an airtight container in the fridge for two to three days.

INGREDIENTS

1½ cups (200 g) finely flaked smoked salmon or lox

1 cup (240 ml) heavy cream

4 eggs

¼ cup (20 g) finely chopped fresh dill

Unrefined sea salt or Himalayan salt, to taste

2 cups (145 g) shredded Swiss cheese or other sharp cheese

SAVORY RICOTTA BUTTERNUT SQUASH TART

This vegetarian, egg-free pie is a perfect example of how to use starch-free thickeners as egg replacements. Here a single teaspoon of psyllium binds the filling together, resulting in a smooth, creamy texture. It took me close to ten trials to get it right, but my family and I are finally satisfied with this version. Whenever I make it, we literally can't stop eating it. If you want to reduce carbs further, or want a simpler version, omit the crust.

Yield: 8 servings

1. Preheat the oven to 350ºF (175 ºC). Place the grated squash, ricotta, heavy cream, psyllium, onion powder, thyme, salt, and nutmeg, if using, into a medium bowl. Mix well and set aside.

2. Prepare the pie crust and prebake it (see page 59). After prebaking, pour in the filling and level the surface with a rubber spatula. Bake for 30 minutes, or until golden brown and completely set. Remove from the oven, let cool slightly, and serve warm.

INGREDIENTS

2 cups (250 g) grated butternut squash flesh

⅔ cup (160 g) ricotta cheese

¼ cup (60 ml) heavy cream

1 teaspoon psyllium husk powder

1 teaspoon onion powder

1 teaspoon dried thyme

1 teaspoon unrefined sea salt or Himalayan salt, or to taste

¼ teaspoon freshly grated nutmeg (optional)

1 Sugar-Free, Starch-Free Pie Crust (page 59)

NOTE: My parents love to serve crushed lingonberries alongside this pie. If you can't find lingonberries, use crushed cranberries instead: You can sweeten them with liquid stevia or powdered erythritol if the tartness of plain cranberries is too much for you.

NUTRITION INFO

WITH CRUST

IN TOTAL:

67.1 g protein;
215.9 g fat;
52.0 g net carbs;
2420 kcal

PER SLICE,
IF 8 SLICES IN TOTAL:

8.4 g protein;
27.0 g fat;
6.5 g net carbs;
302 kcal

QUICK GLUTEN-FREE MICROWAVE PIZZA

Yield: 2 servings

Need a quick fix for dinner? This microwave pizza will do the trick. Thanks to nutritious almond flour and fiber-rich psyllium, plus hearty toppings, this healthy starch-free pizza is sure to satisfy your craving. Feel free to use any leftover veggies and meats you have in the fridge. This pizza is enough for one hungry person, or for two moderately hungry people.

1. Prepare the crust. Mix the almond flour, psyllium, and baking powder in a small bowl. Add the egg and stir with a spoon until a smooth batter forms. Pour the batter on a microwave-safe plate and spread with a spoon until you have a ¼-inch (6 mm) thick layer. Place the plate in the microwave oven and bake on high for 1 minute 30 seconds, or until done.

2. Prepare the sauce. Remove the crust from the microwave and spread the tomato paste evenly over it. Then sprinkle the oregano and onion powder evenly over the tomato paste.

3. Prepare the toppings. Sprinkle the ham and the pepperoni on the crust and top with the cheese. Bake, covered, in the microwave on high for 2 minutes, or until the cheese is bubbly. Let cool for a couple of minutes, then serve.

INGREDIENTS

FOR THE CRUST:

¼ cup (24 g) almond flour

½ teaspoon psyllium husk powder

¼ teaspoon aluminum-free baking powder

1 egg

FOR THE SAUCE:

1½ tablespoons (24 g) unsweetened tomato paste

½ teaspoon dried oregano

Pinch onion powder

TIP: For even easier version, use ready-made sugar-free pizza sauce. (Always read the label to be sure that it doesn't contain food additives.)

FOR THE TOPPINGS:

½ cup (70 g) chopped ham (preferably nitrite-free)

⅓ cup (40 g) chopped pepperoni

1 cup (100 g) shredded mozzarella cheese

NUTRITION INFO

IN TOTAL:

57.7 g protein;
68.5 g fat;
7.2 g net carbs;
875 kcal

PER SERVING,
IF 2 SERVINGS IN TOTAL:

28.9 g protein;
34.2 g fat;
3.6 g net carbs;
438 kcal

FABULOUS PIZZA FOCACCIA FOR THE WHOLE FAMILY

When you're using starch-free real-food ingredients, a little bit goes a long way. And this pizza focaccia is proof: Just a small slice is sure to fill you up. This is a basic version, so go ahead and pretty it up with more toppings of your choice, such as ham, salami, pepperoni, bell pepper, olives, or sliced tomatoes. You can also replace the dried oregano with fresh basil leaves, but do add them after baking, as basil loses its taste if baked or dried.

INGREDIENTS

FOR THE FOCACCIA CRUST:

2 cups (230 g) almond flour

¼ cup (20 g) unflavored grass-fed whey protein

¼ cup (25 g) egg white protein

2 teaspoons aluminum-free baking powder

1 teaspoon unrefined sea salt or Himalayan salt, or to taste

4 eggs

¼ cup (60 ml) light olive oil

OTHER INGREDIENTS:

½ cup (120 ml) sugar-free pizza sauce

3 cups (300 g) shredded mozzarella cheese

1 tablespoon (3 g) dried oregano

Yield: 4 to 6 servings

1. Preheat the oven to 350°F (175°C). Line a baking sheet with parchment paper.

2. First, prepare the crust. Place the almond flour, whey protein, egg white protein, baking powder, and salt in a medium bowl. Mix well and set aside.

3. Place the eggs and the olive oil in a large bowl. Beat with an electric mixer until smooth, about 1 minute. Add the dry ingredients and mix again until smooth, about 1 minute. Pour the batter on the lined baking sheet and spread into a ⅓-inch (8.5 mm) thick layer. Prebake for 10 minutes.

4. When done, remove the crust from the oven and spread the pizza sauce evenly over it. Top with the cheese and oregano. Bake for 15 minutes, or until the cheese is bubbly and golden brown. Cut into pieces and serve immediately.

TIP: Can't find egg white protein? No problem: Use only whey protein, and increase the amount to ½ cup (40 g).

VARIATION: For the ultimate focaccia, make the focaccia crust and spread it on the baking sheet as directed. But before baking, brush the surface with extra-virgin olive oil, sprinkle with fresh rosemary needles and sea salt, and bake as directed. Superb!

NUTRITION INFO

IN TOTAL:

198.1 g protein;
256.4 g fat;
44.2 g net carbs;
3277 kcal

PER SERVING,
IF 4 SERVINGS IN TOTAL:

49.5 g protein;
64.1 g fat;
11.0 g net carbs;
819 kcal

PER SERVING,
IF 6 SERVINGS IN TOTAL:

33.0 g protein;
42.7 g fat;
7.4 g net carbs;
546 kcal

FUSS-FREE, STARCH-FREE LASAGNA

Say hello to the ultimate low-sugar lasagna! This version has no starch or gluten, but it sure is big on nutrients and flavor. And once you try it, it'll become one of your dinnertime staples. No time to bake lasagna tonight? Never fear: The Bolognese sauce alone makes an easy dinner when paired with starch-free pasta and a fresh green salad.

TIP: If the Alfredo sauce is still too thin after adding the egg, place it in a saucepan and bring to a boil, constantly mixing, until the sauce thickens.

INGREDIENTS

FOR THE BOLOGNESE SAUCE:

1 tablespoon (14 g) grass-fed butter

2 tablespoons (4 g) Italian seasoning

1 medium onion, finely chopped

2 garlic cloves, minced

12 ounces (340 g) ground beef

1 teaspoon unrefined sea salt, or to taste

1½ cups (350 ml) unsweetened tomato sauce

¼ cup (65 g) unsweetened tomato paste

FOR THE ALFREDO SAUCE

¾ cup (180 ml) heavy cream

1½ cups (110 g) freshly grated Parmesan cheese

OTHER INGREDIENTS

1 large zucchini (about 1 pound, or 450 g)

1 egg

2 cups (200 g) shredded mozzarella cheese

Yield: 6 servings

1. Preheat the oven to 350°F (175°C).

2. First, prepare the Bolognese sauce. Heat a skillet over medium heat. Add the butter and let it melt. Then add the Italian seasoning, onion, and garlic and cook, stirring, for a couple of minutes until the onion starts to turn translucent. Then add the meat and cook, stirring constantly, crumbling the meat with the back of your spoon or spatula. Add the salt, tomato sauce, and tomato paste and mix well. Reduce the heat and let simmer, covered, for 15 minutes, stirring occasionally. Remove from the heat and set aside.

3. Prepare the Alfredo sauce. Place the heavy cream in a small saucepan and bring to a boil. Add the Parmesan cheese and stir well. Cook until the cheese is melted and the sauce has thickened slightly. Remove from the heat and set aside.

4. Slice the zucchini lengthwise into thin slices and set aside.

5. In a small bowl, combine the Alfredo sauce and the egg and mix well.

6. Spread ½ cup of the Bolognese sauce over the bottom of a 2-quart (2 L) baking dish. Lay half of the zucchini slices on the sauce so that they cover it completely. Spread half of the Alfredo sauce mixture over the zucchini slices. Top with half of the remaining Bolognese sauce, followed by 1 cup (100 g) shredded mozzarella cheese.

7. Lay the rest of the zucchini slices on the shredded mozzarella and top with the rest of the Alfredo sauce. Then spread the rest of the meat sauce on top, and sprinkle with the remaining mozzarella cheese. Bake in the preheated oven for 40 minutes or until golden and bubbly. Let stand for 10 minutes before serving. Best when cooled, refrigerated, and reheated.

NOTE: For easier preparation, make the Bolognese sauce from The Easiest Spaghetti Bolognese on page 134.

NUTRITION INFO

IN TOTAL:

189.4 g protein;
196.7 g fat;
43.5 g net carbs;
2716 kcal

PER SERVING,
IF 6 SERVINGS IN TOTAL:

31.6 g protein;
32.8 g fat;
7.2 g net carbs;
453 kcal

FIVE-INGREDIENT ROASTED MACKEREL WITH THYME AND LEMON

Since it's packed with heart-healthy omega-3 fats, mackerel is one of the most nutritious types of fish on the market. It tastes heavenly when it's roasted in the oven, as in this simple recipe. Serve it with lemon wedges, as their bright, sharp acidity contrasts so well with the hot, oily fish.

INGREDIENTS

4 small (about ½ pound, or 230 g, each) or 2 large (about 1 pound, or 450 g, each) whole mackerels, gutted and cleaned

2 teaspoons unrefined sea salt or Himalayan salt

2 tablespoons (28 ml) extra-virgin olive oil

2 organic lemons: 1 sliced, 1 cut into wedges

40 sprigs fresh thyme

Yield: 4 servings

1. Preheat the oven to 400°F (200°C). Make 4 slashes to each side of the mackerel with a sharp knife. Rub the mackerel with salt and olive oil both inside and outside. Stuff the mackerels with the lemon slices and thyme sprigs. For small mackerel, use five thyme sprigs per mackerel; for large ones, use ten sprigs.

2. Place the fish on a roasting pan and roast for 25 minutes, or until the eyes are white and the fish flakes easily with a fork. Don't overbake, as the fish dries out quickly.

3. While the fish is roasting, remove the leaves from the rest of the thyme sprigs. Discard the stems. When the fish is done, remove it from the oven and serve sprinkled with the thyme leaves and garnished with the lemon wedges.

NUTRITION INFO

IN TOTAL:
191.2 g protein;
59.5 g fat;
0.4 g net carbs;
1302 kcal

PER SERVING,
IF 4 SERVINGS IN TOTAL:
47.8 g protein;
14.9 g fat;
0.1 g net carbs;
326 kcal

BETTER THAN MACARONI AND CHEESE

Looking for filling, low-sugar comfort food your whole family will love? Here's the answer. This creamy, starch-free main is perfect for chilly winter evenings—or whenever you need the dinnertime equivalent of a warm blanket and a hug. It's highly tummy-friendly, too, since it replaces wheat-filled pasta with oh-so-nutritious cauliflower. And that means it won't spike your blood sugar. What's not to like?

INGREDIENTS

1 cup (240 ml) heavy cream

2 eggs

1 teaspoon unrefined sea salt or Himalayan salt, or to taste

teaspoons dry mustard (that is, mustard powder or ground mustard seeds)

½ teaspoon onion powder

¼ teaspoon garlic powder

2 cups (190 g) shredded cheddar cheese

4 cups (565 g) precooked (crisp), cauliflower, chopped into ¼-inch (6 mm) chunks

1 cup (100 g) shredded mozzarella cheese

¼ cup (30 g) almond flour

Yield: 6 servings

1. Preheat the oven to 400°F (200°C).

2. Combine the cream, eggs, salt, mustard, onion powder, and garlic powder in a large saucepan. Heat over medium heat, constantly and carefully stirring with a wire whisk until the mixture starts to thicken. When this happens, reduce the heat to a minimum and add 1½ cups (143 g) of the cheddar cheese. Mix until all the cheese is melted, then add the cauliflower and mix well again.

3. Transfer the mixture to a greased baking dish. Sprinkle the remaining cheddar cheese, all the mozzarella cheese, and the almond flour evenly on top. Bake for 25 minutes, until the top is golden brown and the cheese is bubbly. Let stand for 10 minutes and then serve.

NUTRITION INFO

IN TOTAL:

119.6 g protein;
204.6 g fat;
23.1 g net carbs;
2412 kcal

PER SERVING,
IF 6 SERVINGS IN TOTAL:

19.9 g protein;
34.1 g fat;
3.8 g net carbs;
402 kcal

FIVE-INGREDIENT MOZZARELLA CHICKEN WINGS

I've done plenty of experimenting with recipes for chicken wings, and this one is definitely the winner. It's a bit messy to eat—but that's half the fun, of course. This version is kid-friendly, so it isn't spicy, but if you want to kick up the heat, go ahead and add a little cayenne pepper. If you're expecting guests, these wings make great appetizers, too. (Just be sure to provide extra napkins!)

INGREDIENTS

1½ pounds (680 g) chicken wings

¼ cup (60 ml) light olive oil

7 ounces (200 g) shredded mozzarella cheese

2 teaspoons onion powder

2 teaspoons paprika

1 teaspoon unrefined sea salt or Himalayan salt, or to taste

Yield: 4 servings

1. Preheat the oven to 450°F (230°C).

2. Place the chicken wings and the oil in a large bowl and toss well. Place the oiled chicken wings in a large glass or ceramic baking dish. If there's any oil left in the bowl, pour it over the chicken.

3. Place the mozzarella, onion powder, paprika, and salt, in a medium bowl. Mix well. Sprinkle the mozzarella mixture evenly on the chicken wings and bake for 15 to 20 minutes, or until the juices run clear. Enjoy hot—but don't burn yourself!

NUTRITION INFO

IN TOTAL:
170.6 g protein;
173.1 g fat;
1.2 g net carbs;
2245 kcal

PER SERVING,
IF 4 SERVINGS IN TOTAL:
42.6 g protein;
43.3 g fat;
0.3 g net carbs;
561 kcal

STARCH-FREE WIENER SCHNITZELS

This one's a real European classic—but my gluten-free, starch-free version is so much healthier than the original. (Feel free to make a batch of the breading mixture and keep it on hand as a pantry staple to use for breading chicken, fish, veggies, or cheese. The possibilities are endless!) Serve these schnitzels garnished with anchovies, capers, and lemon slices, plus some oven-baked turnip or rutabaga fries on the side.

INGREDIENTS

FOR THE BREADING MIXTURE:

1 cup (115 g) almond flour

1 tablespoon (9 g) psyllium husk powder

1 teaspoon onion powder

1 teaspoon unrefined sea salt or Himalayan salt

1 pinch ground white pepper

OTHER INGREDIENTS:

2 eggs

4 veal medallions, pork chops, or chicken breasts (12 ounces, or 340 g, in total)

1 stick (8 tablespoons [4 ounces], or 115 g) grass-fed butter or lard, for frying

Yield: 4 servings

1. Combine the ingredients for the breading in a shallow bowl. Set aside.

2. Place the eggs in a separate shallow bowl and mix gently with a fork. Set aside.

3. Pound the meat into ¼-inch (6 mm) thick cutlets, working from the center of the meat outward.

4. Heat a skillet over medium-high heat and add the butter. Take one cutlet and dip it in the egg so that it's completely covered. Then dip it immediately into the breading mixture so that it's completely covered. (You can gently press the breading into the cutlet to help it stick.) Place the breaded cutlet in the skillet and fry until cooked through and golden brown, approximately 4 minutes per side. Flip only once during cooking.

5. Repeat this process with the rest of the cutlets and serve immediately, with turnip or rutabaga fries.

NUTRITION INFO

IN TOTAL:
16.1 g protein;
47.7 g fat;
6.7 g net carbs;
524 kcal

SKINNY TUNA PASTA WITH SHIRATAKI NOODLES

You're starving, and you're just cooking for one tonight. What to do? Skip processed convenience foods, and treat yourself to this fresh, light tuna pasta instead. It's both protein-rich and packed with vegetables, and it's very low-starch, thanks to the shirataki noodles, which are virtually calorie-free. And a final squeeze of fresh lemon juice plus a scattering of fiery red pepper flakes really put a spring in its step.

INGREDIENTS

2.9-ounce (80 g) can tuna in olive oil, not drained

½ small onion, finely chopped

1 clove garlic, crushed

2 sun-dried tomato halves, finely chopped

4 medium canned, drained artichoke hearts, chopped

1 package (7 ounces, or 200 g) shirataki pasta of your preferred shape, rinsed and drained

½ teaspoon unrefined sea salt or Himalayan salt, or to taste

2 teaspoons freshly squeezed lemon juice

1 tablespoon (15 ml) extra-virgin olive oil

Red pepper flakes, to taste

Yield: 1 serving

1. Drain the tuna and reserve the oil. Heat a skillet over medium-high heat. (Avoid high heat, as it encourages the olive oil to splatter.) Add the olive oil from the drained tuna, plus the onion, garlic, sun-dried tomatoes, and the artichoke hearts. Cook, stirring occasionally, until the onion is translucent, about 5 minutes.

2. Add the shirataki pasta and the salt and stir well. Then add the tuna, mix gently, and heat until piping hot, but don't cook. Place on a serving plate, drizzle with the lemon juice and the olive oil, and top with the red pepper flakes. Serve immediately.

QUICK CHICKEN FAJITA PASTA

Craving the flavors of chicken fajitas, minus the carbs and sugar? Amazingly, this creamy, spiced pasta is both starch- and dairy-free, and it's a snap to make, because it relies on just a handful of store-cupboard staples. If you can't find shirataki pasta, replace it with zoodles (that is, spiralized zucchini). Either way, it's a weeknight winner.

INGREDIENTS

2 tablespoons (28 ml) light olive oil

2 teaspoons homemade fajita seasoning mix (see sidebar)

½ small onion, finely chopped

1 garlic clove, finely chopped

½ green bell pepper, chopped

4 ounces (115 g) chicken breast, chopped into bite-size pieces

1 tablespoon (16 g) unsweetened tomato paste

¼ cup (60 ml) coconut cream

1 package (7 ounces, or 200 g) shirataki pasta (fettucine-style, if possible), rinsed and drained

Unrefined sea salt or Himalayan salt and freshly ground black pepper, to taste

Yield: 1 serving

Heat a skillet over medium-high heat. Add the olive oil, fajita seasoning, onion, and garlic. Mix well and cook until the onion is translucent, approximately 5 minutes. Add the bell pepper and the chicken breast. Cook, stirring constantly, until the chicken is done and the juices run clear. Then add the tomato paste and coconut cream and cook until the sauce is as thick as you like it (the longer the sauce cooks, the thicker it gets). Add the shirataki pasta and mix well. Heat it through, but don't cook. Season with salt and pepper and serve immediately.

HOMEMADE FAJITA SEASONING

1 teaspoon onion powder

1 teaspoon ground cumin

1 teaspoon paprika

½ teaspoon garlic powder

¼ teaspoon cayenne pepper

Mix all the spices together well and store in an airtight container.

NUTRITION INFO

IN TOTAL:
30.9 g protein;
44.3 g fat;
7.0 g net carbs;
536 kcal

THE EASIEST SPAGHETTI BOLOGNESE

Spaghetti Bolognese is a classic comfort food, beloved especially by kids. But starchy spaghetti can raise the roof on your blood sugar levels—and that's never a good thing. Your veins and brains will thank you when you make this low-sugar version, though. It's criminally easy, too, so whip up a batch the next time you need to feed the whole family fast.

INGREDIENTS

FOR THE BOLOGNESE SAUCE:

Oil or butter for frying

2 pounds (910 g) ground beef

3 cups (710 ml) unsweetened tomato sauce

1 tablespoon (3 g) dried oregano

2 teaspoons onion powder

½ teaspoon garlic powder

1 teaspoon unrefined sea salt or Himalayan salt, or to taste

Freshly ground black pepper, to taste

OTHER INGREDIENTS:

2 packages (7 ounces, or 200 g, each) shirataki spaghetti

1 ounce (30 g) Parmesan cheese

TIP: Try different starch-free spaghettis. For instance, instead of shirataki, you can use zoodles. They're a good match for Bolognese, because they taste especially crunchy and fresh.

Yield: 4 servings

1. Heat a skillet over medium-high heat. Add the butter or oil and let melt. Add the ground beef and cook, crumbling the meat with the back of your spoon or spatula as you do so. When the meat is done, add the tomato sauce, oregano, onion powder, and garlic powder. Cook, uncovered, until the sauce is reduced and thick. (Lower the heat if the sauce is about to spill over.) Season with salt and pepper.

2. Prepare the shirataki spaghetti according to the package instructions. Divide the spaghetti among four serving plates, and top each with the Bolognese sauce. Grate some Parmesan on top of each serving and serve immediately.

NUTRITION INFO

IN TOTAL:
186.6 g protein;
104.9 g fat;
32.6 g net carbs;
1822 kcal

PER SERVING,
IF 4 SERVINGS IN TOTAL:
46.7 g protein;
26.2 g fat;
8.1 g net carbs;
456 kcal

A-CINCH-TO-MAKE MEATLOAF IN A MUG

This unbelievably juicy meatloaf is so much easier to make than the classic version—no mess involved. The secret ingredient? An egg, which acts as a binder and guarantees a deliciously moist result. And it's ready in no time, so it's the perfect choice for a weeknight dinner-for-one. Serve it with fresh salad and starch-free bread on the side for a full meal, then treat yourself to a low-sugar dessert.

Yield: 1 serving

Combine all the ingredients in a bowl and mix well. Transfer the mixture to a microwave-safe 8-ounce (230 ml) mug. Microwave at 250 watts for 6 to 8 minutes, checking the meatloaf after a couple minutes and adjusting the total cooking time according to your microwave oven. Don't overcook, otherwise the meatloaf becomes too dry. Let cool slightly and serve.

INGREDIENTS

4 ounces (115 g) ground beef

1 tablespoon (15 g) Five-Ingredient Sugar-Free Ketchup (page 39)

1 egg

3 tablespoons (23 g) shredded mozzarella cheese

½ teaspoon dried oregano

¼ teaspoon unrefined sea salt or Himalayan salt, or to taste

TIP: For extra flavor, add one slice of cooked, crumbled bacon to the other ingredients before mixing.

NUTRITION INFO

IN TOTAL:
34.5 g protein;
21.3 g fat;
0.9 g net carbs;
334 kcal

VEGETARIAN EGGPLANT CURRY WITH CAULI BASMATI RICE

A veritable kaleidoscope of tastes and textures, this dish contrasts soft, tender eggplant with crisp fennel and crunchy celery, all bathed in a coconutty cream sauce. Partner it with a batch of Cauli Basmati Rice, a healthy version of traditional, starch-filled basmati rice and an ideal match for all sorts of Asian dishes, such as curries and stir-fries.

TIP: Not a fan of fennel? Don't worry! Its taste is very mild and subtle in this dish. But feel free to replace the fennel or celery with other nonstarchy vegetables such as zucchini, squash, green bell pepper, carrot matchsticks, or shredded cabbage, if you like.

INGREDIENTS

FOR THE VEGETARIAN EGGPLANT CURRY:

Oil or butter for frying

1 to 2 tablespoons (15 to 30 g) green Thai curry paste

1 small onion, chopped

13.5-ounce (400 ml) can coconut milk

1 medium eggplant, diced

1 small fennel bulb, shredded

2 celery stalks, sliced into ¼-inch (6 mm) slices

2 tablespoons (28 ml) fish sauce

1 tablespoon (15 ml) freshly squeezed lime juice

1 tablespoon (10 g) erythritol-based brown sugar substitute (optional)

FOR THE CAULI BASMATI RICE:

1 pound (450 g) cauliflower

1 teaspoon cumin seeds

2 tablespoons (1 ounce, or 30 g) grass-fed butter or olive oil

⅓ cup (60 g) frozen green peas

Unrefined sea salt or Himalayan salt, to taste

Yield: 4 servings

1. Prepare the Vegetarian Eggplant Curry. Place a skillet over medium heat. Add the oil or butter and let it get hot. Add the curry paste and heat for 30 seconds, constantly stirring. Add the onion and cook, stirring occasionally, until translucent, about 5 minutes. (Reduce the heat if the onion is about to brown.)

2. Add the coconut milk and bring to a boil and then add the eggplant to the skillet. Cook, covered, for 10 minutes or until tender. (Hint: While the eggplant is cooking, you can start preparing the Cauli Basmati Rice. See step 4.)

3. Add the fennel and the celery to the skillet. Cook, uncovered, for 5 minutes or until crisp-tender. Add the fish sauce, lime juice, and sweetener, if using, and cook, uncovered, for 1 minute. Remove from the heat and serve with Cauli Basmati Rice.

4. Prepare the Cauli Basmati Rice. Process the cauliflower in a food processor until a ricelike consistency is achieved.

5. Heat a skillet over high heat. Add the cumin seeds and heat for 30 seconds until fragrant, stirring all the time. (Don't let the seeds burn.) Set aside.

6. Reduce the heat to medium-low. Melt the butter (or add the oil) in the skillet and then add the cauliflower. Mix well so that the cauliflower is completely coated. Cover and let simmer for 5 to 10 minutes, or until the cauliflower is crisp-tender. (Don't let it get too soft.) If it starts to brown, add a tablespoon or two (15 to 28 ml) of water and mix well. Add the peas and mix well. Season with salt. Let stand, covered, until the peas have defrosted and are warmed through. Mix well and serve immediately with Vegetarian Eggplant Curry, above.

NUTRITION INFO

IN TOTAL:
38.8 g protein;
112.1 g fat;
54.6 g net carbs;
1383 kcal

PER SERVING,
IF 4 SERVINGS IN TOTAL:
9.7 g protein;
28.0 g fat;
13.7 g net carbs;
346 kcal

FOR THE VEGETARIAN
EGGPLANT CURRY

IN TOTAL:
26.9 g protein;
86.4 g fat;
38.8 g net carbs;
1039 kcal

PER SERVING,
IF 4 SERVINGS IN TOTAL:
6.7 g protein;
21.6 g fat;
9.7 g net carbs;
260 kcal

FOR THE CAULI
BASMATI RICE

IN TOTAL:
11.9 g protein;
25.7 g fat;
15.8 g net carbs;
344 kcal

PER SERVING,
IF 4 SERVINGS IN TOTAL:
3.0 g protein;
6.4 g fat;
4.0 g net carbs;
86 kcal

CAULI RICE SEAFOOD PAELLA

You don't have to give up Spanish-style paella just because you're eating low-sugar. This version replaces the rice with cauli rice, but it's just as good—and it's an entire meal in a single skillet. There are as many recipes for paella as there are cooks, so each one is unique. This is my favorite, but feel free to tweak it to your taste. For instance, my family and I love smoked paprika's distinct flavor, but you can omit it, or replace it with regular paprika, if you're not a fan.

INGREDIENTS

2 tablespoons (28 ml) extra-virgin olive oil

1 medium onion, chopped

4 garlic cloves, crushed

1 large red bell pepper, chopped

8 saffron threads

4 cups (450 g) cauliflower rice

½ cup (120 ml) chicken stock or fish stock

2 tablespoons (32 g) tomato paste

½ teaspoon smoked paprika

½ cup (90 g) frozen green peas

1 pound (450 g) frozen precooked seafood mix

1 teaspoon unrefined sea salt or Himalayan salt, or to taste

Pinch cayenne pepper

Yield: 2 to 4 servings

1. Heat a large skillet over medium-high heat. Add the olive oil, onion, garlic, bell pepper, and saffron. Cook, stirring, until the vegetables are crisp-tender, about 5 minutes. Then add the cauliflower, stock, tomato paste, and smoked paprika and cook, covered, until the cauliflower is crisp-tender, about 5 minutes.

2. Add the frozen peas and the frozen seafood mix. Heat, stirring, until defrosted and completely hot, about 5 to 10 minutes. (Don't cook the seafood or it will become tough.) Season with salt and cayenne pepper and serve immediately.

TIP: Don't want to spend money on pricey saffron? Use ¼ teaspoon turmeric instead. You'll get the same rich yellow color, and plenty of health benefits, too, as turmeric is said to have antioxidant and anti-inflammatory properties.

VARIATION: Serve this with mussels, as shown opposite. Rinse and steam them and add just before serving. If you're not a seafood eater, use 1 pound (450 g) cooked and cubed chicken instead of the seafood mix. Or use the same amount of chorizo sausage, or a mix of chorizo and chicken. (Fry the sausage before adding it.)

FOUR-INGREDIENT CREAMY CURRIED CHICKEN SAUCE WITH MASHED CAULIFLOWER

This recipe boggles the mind: How can something so sating—yet so healthy—be so easy to make? Well, cauliflower and heavy cream are your secret weapons here. The heavy cream gets boiled down to make a thick sauce, while cooked, pureed cauliflower takes the place of carb-laden mashed potatoes. (Don't skimp on the cream. Use the whole amount to achieve a thick, rich sauce.)

INGREDIENTS

FOR THE FOUR-INGREDIENT CREAMY CURRIED CHICKEN SAUCE:

2 tablespoons (1 ounce, or 30 g) grass-fed butter

1 teaspoon curry powder

1 pound (450 g) ground chicken

1½ cups (350 ml) heavy cream

1 teaspoon unrefined sea salt or Himalayan salt, or to taste

FOR THE MASHED CAULIFLOWER:

1½ pounds (680 g) cauliflower, chopped into large chunks

2 tablespoons (1 ounce, or 30 g) grass-fed butter

2 tablespoons (28 ml) heavy cream

1 teaspoon unrefined sea salt or Himalayan salt, or to taste

⅓ cup (30 g) freshly grated Parmesan cheese

Yield: 4 servings

1. Prepare the Four-Ingredient Creamy Curried Chicken Sauce. Heat a large skillet over medium-high heat. Add the butter and let it melt. Add the curry powder and cook, stirring, for 30 seconds or until fragrant. Add the ground chicken and cook, constantly stirring and crumbling the meat with the back of your spoon or spatula as you do so. When the chicken is done—the juices should run clear—pour in the cream. Cook over high heat, stirring constantly, until the sauce is reduced and thick. (Be careful not to let the cream spill over.) Season with salt.

2. While the sauce is cooking, prepare the mashed cauliflower. Boil the cauliflower in a large pot of water until tender and drain well. (Discard the cooking water.) Add the butter, cream, salt, and Parmesan and puree until smooth, preferably with an immersion blender. Add more cream if you prefer a runnier consistency and mix well. Serve immediately, topped with the chicken sauce.

NUTRITION INFO

IN TOTAL:
113.7 g protein;
208.6 g fat;
26.9 g net carbs;
2443 kcal

PER SERVING,
IF 4 SERVINGS IN TOTAL:
28.4 g protein;
52.2 g fat;
6.7 g net carbs;
611 kcal

FOUR-INGREDIENT CREAMY
CURRIED CHICKEN SAUCE

IN TOTAL:
91.7 g protein;
163.9 g fat;
10.9 g net carbs;
1886 kcal

PER SERVING,
IF 4 SERVINGS IN TOTAL:
22.9 g protein;
41.0 g fat;
2.7 g net carbs;
472 kcal

MASHED CAULIFLOWER

IN TOTAL:
22.0 g protein;
44.7 g fat;
16.0 g net carbs;
557 kcal

PER SERVING,
IF 4 SERVINGS IN TOTAL:
5.5 g protein;
11.2 g fat;
4.0 g net carbs;
139 kcal

EASY CAULI RICE MUSHROOM AND PARMESAN RISOTTO

Traditional risotto has two major drawbacks: It requires time and skill to perfect, and the starchy arborio rice from which it's made isn't very healthy. This version is both good for you and easy to make. Don't be put off by the nutritional yeast; it's a natural, nutrient-rich flavor enhancer that adds a cheesy taste to dishes. If you don't have any, add another ¼ cup (20 g) of grated Parmesan.

Yield: 2 to 4 servings

1. Heat a large skillet over medium-high heat and melt the butter in it. Add the mushrooms and cook, stirring occasionally, until all the liquid has evaporated and the mushrooms are tender. Then add the chicken stock, white wine, nutritional yeast, onion powder, and garlic powder and cook, uncovered, until the liquid has reduced by half.

2. Now add the cauliflower and cook, stirring constantly, until crisp-tender, about 5 minutes. Add ¾ cup (60 g) Parmesan and stir until melted. Season with salt and white pepper.

3. Divide the risotto between two serving plates and sprinkle the remaining Parmesan on top of each serving. Serve immediately.

INGREDIENTS

2 tablespoons (1 ounce, or 30 g) grass-fed butter

4 cups (280 g) button mushrooms, chopped

½ cup (120 ml) chicken stock or vegetable stock

¼ cup (60 ml) dry white wine

1 tablespoon (5 g) nutritional yeast

1 teaspoon onion powder

¼ teaspoon garlic powder

4 cups (450 g) cauliflower rice

¾ cup plus ¼ cup (60 g plus 20 g) freshly grated Parmesan cheese, divided

½ teaspoon unrefined sea salt or Himalayan salt, or to taste

Pinch freshly ground white pepper

VARIATION: Want to make this dish even more satisfying? Add 1 cup (140 g) cooked and cubed chicken along with the cauliflower.

NUTRITION INFO

IN TOTAL:
43.7 g protein;
48.6 g fat;
12.6 g net carbs;
702 kcal

PER SERVING,
IF 2 SERVINGS IN TOTAL:
21.9 g protein;
24.3 g fat;
6.3 g net carbs;
351 kcal

PER SERVING,
IF 4 SERVINGS IN TOTAL:
10.9 g protein;
12.1 g fat;
3.2 g net carbs;
176 kcal

TASTY TACO CASSEROLE

Ever checked the ingredient list on that packet of store-bought taco seasoning? Lots of them are full of sugar and starch, so they're off-limits if you're eating low-sugar. But when you make your own homemade taco seasoning—with just five ingredients!—you can be sure that it's clean and sugar-free. It's ideal in this punchy, cheesy, kid-friendly casserole.

NUTRITION INFO

IN TOTAL:
313.4 g protein;
283.4 g fat;
33.7 g net carbs;
3954 kcal

PER SERVING,
IF 8 SERVINGS IN TOTAL:
39.2 g protein;
35.4 g fat;
4.2 g net carbs;
494 kcal

INGREDIENTS

FOR THE TACO SEASONING:

2 tablespoons (15 g) chili powder

1½ tablespoons (11 g) ground cumin

1½ teaspoons onion powder

1 teaspoon garlic powder

½ teaspoon dried oregano

OTHER INGREDIENTS:

Oil or butter for frying

2 pounds (910 g) ground beef

15-ounce (425 g) can green beans, drained

16-ounce (450 g) can diced tomatoes

2 teaspoons unrefined sea salt or Himalayan salt, or to taste

6 cups (240 g) cubed Easy Fluffy Bread (page 53)

4 cups (380 g) shredded mild cheddar cheese

TIP: The taco seasoning is a little spicy. If you're making this dish for kids, you can replace 1 tablespoon (7 g) of the chili powder with paprika.

VARIATION: You can also use half a batch of Just Like Tortilla Chips (page 145) in place of the bread cubes.

Yield: 8 servings

1. Place all taco seasoning ingredients into a small jar with a tightly fitting lid. Close the lid, and shake until well mixed.

2. Prepare the meat sauce. Heat a large skillet over medium-high heat. Add the oil or butter. When hot, add the ground beef and cook. When the meat is browned, add the taco seasoning, green beans, and diced tomatoes. Mix well. Reduce the heat to low, and let simmer until the sauce has thickened, about 20 minutes. Season with salt, mix well, and set aside.

3. Preheat the oven to 350°F (175 °C). Lay half of the bread cubes evenly in the bottom of a casserole dish. Spread half of the meat sauce on the bread cubes and sprinkle half of the cheese on the meat sauce. Spread the rest of the bread cubes on the cheese, top with the rest of the meat sauce, and, finally, sprinkle the rest of the cheese on top. Bake for 30 minutes, or until the cheese is bubbly and golden brown. Remove from the oven, let stand for 10 minutes, and serve.

CHAPTER 8

SNACKS

Even if you eat three meals a day, hunger can strike when you least expect it. Long, hard days at work or school take their toll on grownups, leading to rumbling bellies and flagging energy levels. And kids, with their little tummies, can't eat huge portions all at once, so they need healthy snacks, too. In the coming pages, you'll find ideas for low-sugar snacks that are convenient for noshing on the go—or for leaving in the fridge for your child to grab after school.

For starters, try my recipe for Two-Ingredient Crackers on page 148. It's based on my all-time favorite sour cream and chive cracker recipe, which is adored by kids and adults alike. (I always pack some in my son's school lunchbox.) Or try the Easy Broccoli "Tater Tots" on page 147 and the Magic Cauliflower Popcorn on page 146. They're big hits with kids, too. You can sate your sweet tooth with the Cinnamon–Roll–Flavored Apple Chips on page 152. These good-for-you treats are sugar- and additive-free, but have all the crunch and comfy-cozy flavor of the store-bought variety.

JUST LIKE TORTILLA CHIPS

Ditch the starchy corn and the food additives. You don't need them to make "tortilla" chips that will satisfy your craving for a crunchy, salty snack. This version is bursting with healthy ingredients and lots of fiber, plus—thanks to the nutritional yeast and the onion powder—plenty of flavor. Try dipping them in a batch of homemade guacamole.

INGREDIENTS

8 ounces (230 g) blanched almonds

¼ cup (45 g) white chia seeds

1 tablespoon (5 g) nutritional yeast

1 teaspoon onion powder

1 teaspoon unrefined sea salt or Himalayan salt, or to taste

2 ounces (60 g) full-fat cream cheese, softened

Yield: about 48 chips

1. Preheat the oven to 210ºF (100ºC). Place the almonds, chia seeds, nutritional yeast, onion powder, and salt in a food processor. Process until the mixture resembles corn meal.

2. Transfer the mixture to a medium bowl. Add the cream cheese and knead until a smooth dough forms. If you can't form the dough into a ball, add more cream cheese.

3. Place the dough on a baking sheet lined with parchment paper. Place another piece of parchment paper on the dough. Using a rolling pin, roll the dough out as thinly as possible. Remove the top piece of parchment paper.

4. Cut the dough with a knife or pizza cutter into squares and then crosswise into triangles. Place in the oven and bake for 50 to 60 minutes, checking frequently to prevent the chips from becoming too dark or burning.

5. Let cool completely, then break into triangles along the precut lines. Store in an airtight container in a cool, dry place for up to one week.

NUTRITION INFO

IN TOTAL:
65.0 g protein;
143.4 g fat;
27.1 g net carbs;
1662 kcal

PER CHIP,
IF 48 CHIPS IN TOTAL:
1.4 g protein;
3.0 g fat;
0.6 g net carbs;
35 kcal

MAGIC CAULIFLOWER POPCORN

Packed with fiber and vitamin C, this cauliflower "popcorn" beats the traditional starch-bomb version in every way. And best of all, it takes just five simple items! There's a magic ingredient at work here, of course: cheddar cheese powder, which makes this popcorn incredibly tasty and impossible to resist. Don't bake the cauliflower for too long, though, as you want to be sure to retain its delicious crunch.

INGREDIENTS

2 pounds (910 g) cauliflower (about 1 large head), chopped into bite-size pieces

1 tablespoon (15 ml) light olive oil

1 teaspoon unrefined sea salt, or to taste

¼ teaspoon garlic powder

⅓ cup (35 g) white cheddar cheese powder

Yield: about 5 cups (500 g)

1. Preheat the oven to 400°F (200°C). Line a baking sheet with parchment paper. Place the cauliflower, olive oil, salt, and garlic powder in a large bowl. Toss until well mixed.

2. Spread the cauliflower on the lined baking sheet in a single layer so that the cauliflower pieces barely touch one other, and bake for 10 minutes.

3. Remove the cauliflower from the oven and pour the hot cauliflower pieces into a large heatproof bowl. (The best way to do this is by grabbing the short ends of the cauliflower-loaded parchment paper and carefully lifting it up to pour the cauliflower right into the bowl. Don't burn yourself!) Add the cheddar cheese powder and toss with a spoon until the cauliflower is completely and evenly covered. Let cool on a cooling rack for a few minutes. Serve warm.

NUTRITION INFO

IN TOTAL:
30.3 g protein;
26.0 g fat;
27.0 g net carbs;
463 kcal

PER 1 CUP (100 G):
6.1 g protein;
5.2 g fat;
5.4 g net carbs;
93 kcal

EASY BROCCOLI "TATER TOTS"

Did you know that just 3½ ounces (100 g) of commercially produced Tater Tots contain about eight sugar cubes? So, if you wouldn't feed your child eight sugar cubes (especially at a single sitting), skip them and make a batch of these addictive-but-nutritious Easy Broccoli "Tater Tots" instead. They're just as good, and far healthier, since there's no nasty sugar in sight.

INGREDIENTS

1 cup (240 g) soft-cooked broccoli, tightly packed

1 cup (100 g) grated mozzarella cheese

½ cup (60 g) almond flour

1 teaspoon psyllium husk powder

1 teaspoon onion powder

1 egg

1 teaspoon unrefined sea salt or Himalayan salt, or to taste

2 tablespoons (28 ml) extra-light olive oil, for brushing

NUTRITION INFO

IN TOTAL:
56.7 g protein;
84.0 g fat;
11.4 g net carbs;
1043 kcal

PER TATER TOT,
IF 16 TATER TOTS IN TOTAL:
3.5 g protein;
5.2 g fat;
0.7 g net carbs;
65 kcal

Yield: about 16 tater tots

1. Preheat the oven to 350°F (175 °C). Line a baking sheet with parchment paper. Place all ingredients in a medium bowl and mix with an electric mixer until smooth.

2. Scoop up 2 tablespoons (28 g) of the mixture. With liberally oiled hands, shape it into a cylindrical or rectangular tater-tot shape. Place the tater tot on the lined baking sheet. Repeat with the remaining broccoli mixture.

3. Brush each tater tot generously with olive oil, then transfer the tray to the oven and bake for 20 minutes, or until golden brown. (Keep an eye on them to prevent them from burning.) Remove from the oven, let cool, and then serve with Five-Ingredient Sugar-Free Ketchup (page 39), Foolproof One-Minute Mayo (page 41), or a sugar-free dip of your choice.

TWO-INGREDIENT CRACKERS

These melt-in-your-mouth crackers are such a healthy alternative to starch-laden store-bought crackers or potato chips. With just two ingredients, they're amazingly simple. They're great on their own, or with just about any kind of low-sugar topping. Try spreading them with flavored cream cheeses (as long as they're made without food additives, of course). Or you can add chopped fresh chives to the dough to make cream cheese and chive crackers.

INGREDIENTS

2 cups (230 g) almond flour

2.5 ounces (70 g) full-fat cream cheese (any flavor)

1 teaspoon unrefined sea salt or Himalayan salt, or to taste (optional)

Yield: about 48 crackers

1. Preheat the oven to 210°F (100°C). Mix all ingredients by hand in a medium bowl. Knead for about half a minute or until a smooth dough forms.

2. Place the dough on a baking sheet lined with parchment paper. Place another piece of parchment paper on top of the dough. Using a rolling pin, roll the dough out as thinly as possible between the two pieces of parchment paper. Then remove the top piece.

3. Use a knife or pizza cutter to cut the dough into squares (or other shapes of your choice). Place in the oven and bake for 50 to 60 minutes, checking frequently to prevent the crackers from becoming too dark or burning. Let cool completely before removing from the baking sheet. Store in an airtight container in a cool, dry place for up to one week.

NUTRITION INFO

IN TOTAL:
54.0 g protein;
131.8 g fat;
23.9 g net carbs;
1498 kcal

PER CRACKER,
IF 48 CRACKERS IN TOTAL:

1.1 g protein;
2.7 g fat;
0.5 g net carbs;
31 kcal

NUTRITION INFO

NOTE: THE EXACT VALUES
DEPEND ON THE NUT MIX USED.

IN TOTAL:
34.2 g protein;
162.2 g fat;
32.2 g net carbs;
1757 kcal

PER ¼ CUP (ABOUT 35 G):
8.6 g protein;
40.5 g fat;
8.0 g net carbs;
439 kcal

BEST BBQ NUTS

These nuts make a great party snack, or an impromptu appetizer for last-minute guests. Don't be surprised, though, if these gems disappear as soon as you serve them, since they're spiced, crunchy, and finger-licking good. During the holidays, you can fill a beautiful glass jar with these nuts and give them as a healthy, delicious gift. Feel free to mix things up by experimenting with different herbs and spices.

INGREDIENTS

8 ounces (230 g) mixed nuts
(such as almonds, blanched hazelnuts, pecans, or macadamia nuts)

1 tablespoon (15 ml) extra-light olive oil

1½ teaspoons salt-free barbecue seasoning

1 teaspoon unrefined sea salt or Himalayan salt, or to taste

1 tablespoon (10 g) erythritol-based brown sugar substitute (optional)

Yield: about 2½ cups (350 g)

1. Preheat the oven to 350°F (175 °C). Line a baking sheet with parchment paper. Place all the ingredients into a resealable freezer bag. Close the bag tightly and shake it well to let the spices and oil cover the nuts evenly. Spread the mixture over the baking sheet into a thin, even layer. Bake for 10 to 12 minutes, or until golden brown. Keep an eye on the nuts as they bake, as they burn very easily.

2. Let the nuts cool completely on the baking sheet and then remove and serve. Store leftovers in an airtight container in a cool, dry place for up to two days.

CINNAMON ROLL–FLAVORED APPLE CHIPS

NOTE: Got leftover sweetener-and-spice mixture? Don't let it go to waste: Sprinkle it on your breakfast yogurt, or spread butter on a slice of Easy Fluffy Bread (page 53) and top it with the sweetener-and-spice mixture, to make instant cinnamon toast.

Finally: There's a healthy way to enjoy cinnamon buns! And the proof's in the pudding—or, in this case, in the Cinnamon Roll–Flavored Apple Chips. Choose the sourest possible apples for the lowest sugar content, then rub them with spices and sweetener and pop them into a warm oven for a few hours. You can get creative with your choice of spices, too. For example, pumpkin pie spice makes a great autumnal treat, and gingerbread seasoning is perfect for the holidays. Don't despair if the chips aren't crisp when they're warm from the oven: Thanks to the erythritol, they'll crisp up after cooling down.

Yield: about 3½ cups (98 g)

1. Preheat the oven to 200°F (90°C). Line two baking sheets with parchment paper. Place the erythritol, cinnamon, and vanilla powder in a small bowl and mix well.

2. Slice the apples as thinly as possible. Discard the seeds.

3. Place the apple slices on the lined baking sheets in a single layer. Using clean hands, rub each slice on both sides with the sweetener-and-spice mixture. Then bake for 4 hours or until crisp, switching the position of the baking sheets halfway through baking. When the slices are crisp, remove the baking sheets. Let the chips cool and then serve. Store leftovers in an airtight container for up to two weeks.

INGREDIENTS

2 tablespoons (16 g) powdered erythritol

½ teaspoon Ceylon cinnamon

¼ teaspoon vanilla powder

2 small Granny Smith apples, or other sour apples

TIP: To make a sweetener-free version, just rub the apple slices with a mixture of cinnamon and vanilla powder.

NUTRITION INFO

IN TOTAL:
0.7 g protein;
0.3 g fat;
23.6 g net carbs;
105 kcal

PER 1 CUP (28 G):
0.2 g protein;
0.1 g fat;
5.9 g net carbs;
26 kcal

CHAPTER 9

DESSERTS

Quitting sugar doesn't mean saying no to dessert. You can still enjoy decadent-tasting sweet treats on a low-sugar lifestyle—except that these versions are actually good for you. Made with natural sweeteners and clean ingredients, the luscious recipes in this chapter are safe for kids and adults alike.

Best of all, they're quick and easy to make. If all you have is a few minutes, try the Quick and Rich Low-Sugar Chocolate Mousse on page 157: Just a couple of spoonfuls will banish your chocolate craving, stat (until next time, that is). If you have a little more time on your hands, whip up the Crunchy One-Bowl, Five-Ingredient Cookies on page 164, or the One-Two-Three-Four-Five Cake on page 160—an easy-to- remember recipe for a basic cake that's especially great for birthdays. Or make a batch of Sugar-Free Natural-Ingredient Gummy Bears (page 168) for your kids and then watch them disappear in mere minutes. Not that you'll sharpen your sweet tooth because all of these recipes are only moderately sweet, to help wean you off of sugary or highly sweetened foods.

EASY SUGAR-FREE VANILLA ICE CREAM

This no-cook recipe makes homemade sugar-free ice cream ridiculously simple. And it's extra-creamy, thanks to a secret ingredient—full-fat sour cream—which also adds a palate-pleasing tang. The hardest part? Waiting for the ice cream to freeze before you dig in. (Please note that this recipe contains raw egg.)

Yield: 4 servings

Place all ingredients in a deep, narrow bowl. First stir well with a spoon to fold in the powdered erythritol and then mix with an electric mixer until thoroughly combined. Pour the mixture into the ice cream maker and let it churn according to the manufacturer's instructions. Serve it immediately after churning for soft-serve ice cream, but if you prefer a harder ice cream, you can freeze it for an hour or so before serving. Store in the freezer for up to two weeks.

INGREDIENTS

1 egg

⅓ cup (43 g) powdered erythritol

10 drops vanilla stevia, or to taste

1 cup (240 ml) heavy cream

8 ounces (230 g) full-fat sour cream

2 teaspoons vanilla extract, or the scraped seeds from one vanilla bean

NUTRITION INFO

IN TOTAL:
19.5 g protein;
130.1 g fat;
17.8 g net carbs;
1320 kcal

PER SERVING,
IF 4 SERVINGS IN TOTAL:
4.9 g protein;
32.5 g fat;
4.4 g net carbs;
330 kcal

QUICK AND RICH LOW-SUGAR CHOCOLATE MOUSSE

Having a busy day? No problem: There's still plenty of time to enjoy a sugar-free dessert. Get your chocolate fix with this mouthwatering—and nutritious—chocolate mousse, which takes just a few minutes to prepare. You can eat it right away if you like, or, to help it set, pop it into the fridge for half an hour or so. (Please note that this recipe contains raw egg.)

Yield: 4 servings

Using an electric mixer, beat the eggs, cocoa powder, erythritol, and salt on high speed until fluffy, about 5 minutes. Add the heavy cream and beat until the mixture reaches a mousse-like consistency, about 5 minutes. Add the vanilla stevia and the rum, if using, and beat until well mixed, about 1 minute. Divide the mousse among four serving bowls and refrigerate for 30 minutes to help it set, if you have time. (If not, go ahead and serve it immediately.) Decorate with grated dark chocolate and whipped cream and serve.

INGREDIENTS

2 eggs

¼ cup (30 g) unsweetened dark cocoa powder

¼ cup (32 g) powdered erythritol

Pinch unrefined sea salt or Himalayan salt

⅔ cup (160 ml) heavy cream

25 drops vanilla stevia

Rum or sugar-free rum flavoring, to taste (optional)

Grated dark chocolate (with a minimum cocoa content of 85 percent) and whipped cream, to serve

TIP: Use natural flavorings to add variation to this dessert, such as orange, cherry, or almond. Flavored stevia can do the trick, too, so feel free to experiment.

FIVE-INGREDIENT HEAVEN AND HELL CHEESECAKE

You won't be able to believe that this sinful-tasting cheesecake is actually good for you. But it's true! With only five natural ingredients, it's a fluffy, no-cheat cheesecake that's so easy to make it's practically foolproof—if you follow the instructions, that is. Don't despair if you see a crater in the middle of the cheesecake when it's time to turn off the heat in the oven: The surface of the cake will even out when it's cooling in the oven.

Yield: 8 servings

1. Preheat the oven to 300°F (150°C). Grease an 8-inch (20 cm) springform pan generously with butter. Combine the cream cheese, sweetener, and sour cream in a medium bowl. Mix until smooth and fluffy, about 5 minutes. Add the eggs one at a time, beating well after each addition. Add the vanilla extract, beat it until well mixed, and then pour the batter into the pan.

2. Place a shallow, ovenproof bowl on the lowest rack. Carefully fill it three-quarters full with boiling water. Place the dish with the batter on the middle oven rack.

3. Bake for 45 minutes, or until the edges are firm but the center is still wobbly. Turn off the heat, but do not remove the cake from the oven: Let it sit in the oven for 1 hour. Remove the cake and let it cool to room temperature before placing it in the fridge for 6 hours or overnight. Bring to room temperature 30 minutes before serving.

INGREDIENTS

Butter (for greasing)

1 pound (450 g) full-fat cream cheese, softened

½ cup (65 g) powdered erythritol

⅓ cup (80 g) full-fat sour cream, at room temperature

2 eggs, at room temperature

1 teaspoon vanilla extract

NOTE: Don't increase the oven temperature for this recipe. If you use a higher temperature, the cake will turn brown and will sink once cooled.

NUTRITION INFO

IN TOTAL:
44.1 g protein;
133.0 g fat;
18.5 g net carbs;
1466 kcal

PER SLICE,
IF 8 SLICES IN TOTAL:
5.5 g protein;
16.6 g fat;
2.3 g net carbs;
183 kcal

GUILT-FREE PUMPKIN PIE

This six-ingredient low-sugar pumpkin pie is a cinch to make. You'll be tempted to eat it the minute it comes out of the oven, but try to resist; leaving it in the fridge overnight to set allows for a deeper, more intense flavor, and improves the texture markedly. And don't forget to serve it with fluffy peaks of (sugar-free) whipped cream!

INGREDIENTS

Butter (for greasing)

15-ounce (425 g) can 100 percent pure pumpkin

1 cup (240 ml) heavy cream

⅔ cup (66 g) erythritol crystals

3 eggs

2 teaspoons pumpkin pie spice, or to taste

1 teaspoon vanilla extract

VARIATION: If you prefer your pumpkin pie with a flaky crust, use the Vegan Sugar-Free, Starch-Free Pie Crust (page 59), adding 2 tablespoons (25 g) powdered erythritol to the dry ingredients. Pour the pumpkin pie filling into the prebaked crust and then continue with the instructions as above.

Yield: 4 to 8 servings

1. Preheat the oven to 350°F (175 °C). Grease a 10-inch (25 cm) pie pan or baking dish generously with butter. Set aside.

2. Place all ingredients in a large bowl and mix with an electric mixer until smooth and free from lumps. Pour the mixture into the greased pie pan and bake for 1 hour, or until the center of the pie appears slightly higher than the edges. Remove and let cool completely.

3. Refrigerate overnight. Slice and serve with a dollop of whipped cream.

NUTRITION INFO

WITHOUT CRUST

IN TOTAL:

36.3 g protein;
103.9 g fat;
20.5 g net carbs;
1180 kcal

PER SLICE,
IF 8 SLICES IN TOTAL:

4.5 g protein;
13 g fat;
2.6 g net carbs;
147 kcal

PER SLICE,
IF 4 SERVINGS IN TOTAL:

10 g protein;
34.8 g fat;
5.1 g net carbs;
375 kcal

WITH CRUST

IN TOTAL:

80.3 g protein;
278.1 g fat;
40.6 g net carbs;
3004 kcal

ONE-TWO-THREE-FOUR-FIVE CAKE

Baking a healthy, sugar-free, gluten-free cake is as easy as counting to five. Serve this small and simple-but-scrumptious cake with jam and cream, or ice it with your favorite sugar-free frosting. It's super-versatile—you can add nuts, dark chocolate chips, sugar-free jam, or flavoring to the batter for extra variation—and it makes the perfect birthday cake, too.

INGREDIENTS

1 cup (115 g) almond flour

2 teaspoons aluminum-free baking powder

3 tablespoons (21 g) coconut flour

4 tablespoons (32 g) powdered erythritol

5 eggs

Yield: 12 to 20 servings

1. Preheat the oven to 350°F (175°C). Combine the almond flour, baking powder, coconut flour, and sweetener in a small bowl. Mix well to break up any lumps.

2. Beat the eggs until fluffy and pale, then fold in the dry ingredients. Mix with a rubber spatula until smooth. Pour the batter into a generously greased 5-inch (10 cm) cake pan. Bake for 30 minutes or until a toothpick inserted into the middle of the cake comes out clean. Remove the cake from the pan, let cool, and serve.

NUTRITION INFO

IN TOTAL:

67.9 g protein;
91.2 g fat;
18.3 g net carbs; 1174
kcal

PER SLICE,
IF 12 SLICES IN TOTAL:

5.7 g protein;
7.6 g fat;
1.5 g net carbs;
98 kcal

PER SLICE,
IF 20 SLICES IN TOTAL:

3.4 g protein;
4.6 g fat;
0.9 g net carbs;
59 kcal

EASY FUDGY BROWNIES

Healthy brownies—that's an oxymoron, right? Nope: These melt-in-your-mouth treats are sinfully irresistible, but they're actually good for you because they're free from grain, sugar, and artificial fats. Instead, they feature real butter, dark chocolate, and fiber-rich coconut flour for the healthiest, richest-tasting result. (Hint: These little gems taste best the day after they're made.)

INGREDIENTS

1 stick (4 ounces, or 115 g) salted grass-fed butter

4 ounces (115 g) dark chocolate (minimum 85 percent cocoa solids)

¼ cup (30 g) coconut flour

2 teaspoons aluminum-free baking powder

⅓ cup (33 g) erythritol crystals

25 drops vanilla stevia

4 eggs

1 cup (115 g) chopped walnuts (optional)

NOTE: Warm the brownies and serve with Easy Sugar-Free Vanilla Ice Cream (page 155). It doesn't get any better than that!

TIP: Add ½ cup (85 g) dark chocolate chips (with a minimum cocoa content of 85 percent) to the dough for extra-chocolaty brownies.

Yield: about 12 brownies

1. Preheat the oven to 350°F (175 °C). Place the butter and the chocolate in a small saucepan. Place over medium heat, stirring constantly, until melted. Remove from the heat and set aside.

2. Combine the coconut flour and the baking powder in a small bowl. Mix well and set aside.

3. Combine the melted butter and chocolate mixture, erythritol crystals, and vanilla stevia in a medium bowl. Beat with an electric mixer until smooth. Add the eggs one at a time, beating well after each addition. (Don't worry if the mixture looks separated. It will become smooth after you have added all the eggs.) After adding the last egg, beat the mixture until light and fluffy, about 5 to 10 minutes. Add the coconut flour mixture and beat again until smooth. Fold in the chopped walnuts, if using.

4. Pour the mixture into an 8 x 8-inch (20 x 20 cm) silicone brownie pan or greased glass or ceramic baking dish. Bake for 15 to 20 minutes, or until the edges are firm but the center is still a bit wobbly. Don't overbake. Let cool completely, remove from the pan, and cut into pieces. Store in the fridge, and bring to room temperature 30 minutes before serving.

CRUNCHY ONE-BOWL, FIVE-INGREDIENT COOKIES

It took a little trial and error, but I finally came up with a cookie recipe that my family and I love. The result? Crunchy, buttery, vanilla-flavored cookies with plenty of flavor, but no sugar, starch, or even egg. Need I say more?

INGREDIENTS

1 cup (115 g) almond flour

⅓ cup (30 g) vanilla-flavored grass-fed whey protein

6 tablespoons (3 ounces, or 85 g) unsalted grass-fed butter, softened

3 tablespoons (39 g) erythritol crystals

25 drops vanilla stevia

TIP: Add ⅓ cup (60 g) dark chocolate chips (with a minimum cocoa content of 85 percent) to the dough to make delicious, low-sugar chocolate chip cookies.

Yield: about 16 cookies

1. Preheat the oven to 350°F (175°C). Line a baking sheet with parchment paper.

2. Combine all ingredients in a medium bowl. Using clean hands, knead until the mixture is well combined and the dough is smooth and free from clumps. Then shape the dough into small walnut-size balls. Place them on the lined baking sheet and flatten them with wet fingertips.

3. Bake for 5 to 7 minutes, or until golden brown. (Keep an eye on the cookies. They can get too brown very quickly.) Let cool completely before removing from the baking sheet. This is important because the hot cookies are very fragile. When cool, store in an airtight container in a cool, dry place for up to one week.

NUTRITION INFO

IN TOTAL:

46.7 g protein;
1321.6 g fat;
13.9 g net carbs;
1439 kcal

PER COOKIE,
IF 16 COOKIES IN TOTAL:

2.9 g protein;
8.3 g fat;
0.9 g net carbs;
90 kcal

NUTRITION INFO.

IN TOTAL:
19.4 g protein;
32.6 g fat;
5.1 g net carbs;
395 kcal

FLOURLESS FOUR-INGREDIENT PEANUT BUTTER CAKE IN A MUG

When I made this mug cake for my son, he proclaimed, "This is the best cake you have ever made!"—and he doesn't even like peanut butter! That endorsement pretty much says it all when it comes to this incredibly easy, single-serving cake. Make one for your kids (or yourself) the next time they beg for a sweet treat. I bet they'll agree.

Yield: 1 serving

Place all ingredients into a large microwave-safe mug and mix vigorously with a spoon to form a smooth batter. Microwave on high for 1 minute and 30 seconds. Check the cake after 1 minute and adjust the overall cooking time according to your microwave oven. Don't overbake. Let cool until warm and serve.

INGREDIENTS

3 tablespoons (48 g) unsweetened peanut butter

2 tablespoons (26 g) erythritol crystals

1 egg

¼ teaspoon aluminum-free baking powder

¼ teaspoon vanilla extract (optional)

VARIATION: It's easy to vary this one-mug wonder. For peanut butter and chocolate chip cake, add 2 tablespoons (22 g) dark chocolate chips or chopped homemade sugar-free chocolate to the batter and mix well. For a peanut-butter-and-jelly cake, drop 1 tablespoon (15 g) Easy Sugar-Free Strawberry Jam (page 51) into the batter before baking. Use a fork to create a swirl in the batter, then bake.

SUGAR-FREE NATURAL-INGREDIENT GUMMY BEARS

Bursting with brisk citrus flavors, these candies have only natural ingredients, and they contain super-healthy gelatin. That makes them a far cry from the industrially produced store-bought versions. Don't worry if the hot liquid mixture doesn't seem like a lot: It makes a whopping five dozen gummy bears which your kids can enjoy to their hearts' content.

INGREDIENTS

¼ cup (60 ml) freshly squeezed orange juice

¼ cup (32 g) powdered erythritol

2 tablespoons (28 ml) freshly squeezed lemon juice

20 drops lemon stevia

3 tablespoons (21 g) gelatin powder

2 drops 100 percent orange essential oil

TIP: Try different pure fruit juices in place of the orange juice, or experiment with different flavored stevia and various natural flavorings.

Yield: about 60 gummy bears

Place all ingredients in a small saucepan and heat over medium-high heat, stirring constantly. When the gelatin has melted but the mixture is not yet boiling, remove the saucepan from the heat. Pour the liquid into a silicone gummy bear mold. (There are special bottles for this purpose on the market to make the process easier and less messy. Use one of these, if you like.) Place the mold in the refrigerator for 1 to 2 hours, remove the gummy bears from the mold, and store in an airtight container in the fridge for up to one week.

NOTE: Handle the hot candy mixture carefully, as it spills from the bottle easily. These candies are easy to make, but unfortunately the hot liquid means that kids shouldn't help with preparation for safety reasons.

NUTRITION INFO

IN TOTAL:
25.9 g protein;
0.2 g fat;
5.5 g net carbs;
135 kcal

PER GUMMY BEAR,
IF 60 GUMMY BEARS
IN TOTAL:
0.4 g protein;
trace fat;
0.1 g net carbs;
2 kcal

SIX-INGREDIENT CARAMEL GLAZED DONUTS

Break out the donut maker. Soft, pillowy donuts are just a few minutes away! Of course, they're grain- and sugar-free. For a decadent finish, glaze them with my Three-Ingredient Sugar-Free Caramel Glaze on page 47 after they've cooled. Then, get ready to make a second batch: Your family will gobble them up as fast as you can make them.

INGREDIENTS

FOR THE DONUTS:

¼ cup (30 g) coconut flour

2 teaspoons aluminum-free baking powder

3 eggs

⅓ cup (33 g) erythritol crystals

¼ cup (60 ml) heavy cream

2 teaspoons vanilla extract

OTHER INGREDIENTS:

¼ cup (60 ml) melted grass-fed butter, for brushing the donut maker

1 batch Three-Ingredient Sugar-Free Caramel Glaze (page 47)

Yield: about 24 donuts

1. Place the coconut flour and baking powder in a small bowl. Mix well to break up any lumps. Place the rest of the ingredients for the donuts into a medium bowl and whisk well. Gradually whisk the dry ingredients into the wet.

2. Heat the donut maker to medium and brush each dip generously with melted butter. Fill each dip completely with batter and close the lid. Cook for 3 minutes and then open the lid carefully. (Adjust the cooking time according to your donut maker.) Remove the cooked donuts and place on a cooling rack.

3. Repeat the process with the rest of the batter, brushing the dips of the donut maker generously with the melted butter before pouring in the batter.

4. When all donuts have cooled to room temperature, prepare the Three-Ingredient Sugar-Free Caramel Glaze and let it cool to room temperature. Drizzle the glaze over the donuts and let it set. Remove the donuts from the cooling rack. Store in an airtight container in a cool, dry place for up to two days.

NUTRITION INFO

WITH GLAZE

IN TOTAL:
38.1 g protein;
206.4 g fat;
23.2 g net carbs;
2110 kcal

PER DONUT,
IF 24 DONUTS IN TOTAL:
1.6 g protein;
8.6 g fat;
1.0 g net carbs;
88 kcal

WITHOUT GLAZE

IN TOTAL:
30.7 g protein;
68.2 g fat;
11.5 g net carbs;
791 kcal

PER DONUT,
IF 24 DONUTS IN TOTAL:
1.3 g protein;
2.8 g fat;
0.5 g net carbs;
33 kcal

LOW-SUGAR MILK CHOCOLATE

Homemade sugar-free milk chocolate is a great way to satisfy your inner chocoholic—without diving into unhealthy sugar and additives. Just be sure to choose milk powder that contains as little milk sugar as possible. This scaled-back recipe makes just 4 ounces (115 g) of chocolate, so double or triple the ingredients if you're planning to serve a bigger crowd.

INGREDIENTS

¼ cup (30 g) milk powder

3 tablespoons (24 g) powdered erythritol

1 tablespoon (7 g) unsweetened dark cocoa powder

Pinch unrefined sea salt or Himalayan salt

2 ounces (60 g) cocoa butter

20 drops vanilla stevia

TIP: For even lower-sugar milk chocolate (and a vegan, dairy-free version), replace the milk powder with sugar-free coconut milk powder.

NOTE: Don't omit the salt—it's a must. Salt adds a decadent note to the sweet chocolate and rounds out the flavors. Salt is a mandatory ingredient in just about every recipe that calls for chocolate.

Yield: 8 servings

1. Sift the milk powder, erythritol, dark cocoa powder, and salt into a small bowl. (Sifting removes any lumps.) Set aside.

2. Melt the cocoa butter in a small saucepan over low heat, or in the microwave oven in thirty-second spans. Be careful not to let the cocoa butter boil. Add the cocoa butter and vanilla stevia to the cocoa powder mixture and stir well until the mixture is smooth and the erythritol has dissolved. Heat in the microwave or in a saucepan over low heat if the mixture looks grainy. Pour the mixture into preferred chocolate molds and place it in the fridge for 2 to 3 hours to set.

3. When done, store in the fridge in an airtight container for up to one week.

NUTRITION INFO

IN TOTAL:
14.5 g protein;
63.1 g fat;
11.3 g net carbs;
670 kcal

PER ½ OUNCE (14 G):
1.8 g protein;
7.9 g fat;
1.4 g net carbs;
84 kcal

TRULY SUGAR-FREE WHITE CHOCOLATE

Prepare yourself: This is the ultimate sugar-free white chocolate. Sweetened with erythritol and stevia—not a grain of sugar anywhere, naturally—this heavenly treat will be a huge hit with your family. Coconut manna (that is, minced coconut flesh) is the secret ingredient. It yields a rich-yet-subtle flavor. Oh, this goodie is vegan and dairy-free, too, so you can enjoy it freely even if you don't tolerate dairy.

Yield: 10 servings

Melt the cocoa butter and coconut manna in a small saucepan over low heat, or in the microwave oven in thirty-second spans. Be careful not to let the mixture boil. Add the erythritol, stevia, and salt, and mix well. Pour into your favorite chocolate molds and place in the fridge for 2 to 3 hours to set. When done, store in the fridge in an airtight container for up to two weeks.

INGREDIENTS

2 ounces (60 g) cocoa butter

2 ounces (60 g) coconut manna

3 tablespoons (24 g) powdered erythritol

25 drops vanilla stevia

Pinch unrefined sea salt or Himalayan salt

NOTE: Use this sugar-free white chocolate in exactly the same way as you'd use its sugary counterpart. For instance, you can create white chocolate chips from it and use them in cookies—such as the Crunchy One-Bowl, Five-Ingredient Cookies on page 164.

NUTRITION INFO

IN TOTAL:
4.0 g protein;
97.1 g fat;
4.3 g net carbs;
915 kcal

PER 1/2 OUNCE (14 G):
0.4 g protein;
9.7 g fat;
0.4 g net carbs;
92 kcal

CHAPTER 10

DRINKS

Brimming with sugar, additives, and colorings, store-bought soft drinks, lemonades, and iced teas are definite no-nos when you're kicking the sugar habit. Luckily, it's simple to prepare healthy, sugar-free versions of all of these and more, using clean, natural ingredients that are suitable for both kids and grownups. On hot and sweaty summer days, you'll want to make a batch or two of Basic Sugar-Free Iced Tea (page 174), Guilt-Free Lemonade (page 175), or Apple Pie–Infused Water (page 177). Or serve up a round of my Mighty Mint Lassi (page 178) or Supreme Orange Creamsicle Shake (page 179) for a refreshing after-lunch treat.

When the weather turns cool, look to hot drinks such as the Creamy No-Sugar Hot Chocolate on page 180, or the Healthy PSL on page 182. Both are scrumptious, warming, and nutritious. And as for the holidays, you can rest assured that my silky-as-mousse Rich Sugar-Free Eggnog (page 183) will delight you and your guests. It's so good that they'll never guess it's sugar-free. Cheers!

BASIC SUGAR-FREE ICED TEA

Yield: 6 to 8 servings

If warm summer days make you crave a pitcher of iced tea, throw out that yucky powdered stuff and try this version instead. To help you quit sugar, it's not overly sweet, but it's still plenty refreshing. Adding a pinch of baking soda to the tea while brewing guarantees a smooth taste—minus the bitterness that's typical of black tea. (Baking soda is highly alkaline, so it helps neutralize the bitter acids in black tea.) Use this recipe as a template and experiment with different types of tea and stevia flavors. I bet you'll come up with dozens of unique combinations.

1. Put the baking soda into a small bowl and add the tea bags. Pour in the boiling water, add the erythritol, and mix gently. Let the tea steep for 20 minutes.

2. Remove the tea bags, squeezing them carefully to retain all the liquid. Discard the teabags.

3. Transfer the mixture to a 64-ounce (1.9 L) glass pitcher. Add the ice-cold water, lemon juice, and lemon stevia, and mix well. Adjust the taste by adding more lemon stevia or unflavored stevia, if you prefer a sweeter iced tea. Fill the pitcher with ice cubes and serve.

INGREDIENTS

1 pinch baking soda

4 bags orange pekoe or other good-quality black tea

1 cup (240 ml) boiling water

½ cup (100 g) erythritol crystals

5 cups (1.2 L) ice-cold water

¼ cup (60 ml) freshly squeezed lemon juice

40 drops lemon stevia

Ice cubes for serving

TIP: Can't find lemon stevia? Just place 2 teaspoons freshly grated lemon zest into a mesh tea ball and steep it together with the tea. Remove it along with the tea bags, and increase the amount of erythritol to ¾ cup (155 g).

NUTRITION INFO

IN TOTAL:
0.4 g protein;
0.1 g fat;
1.6 g net carbs;
41 kcal

PER SERVING,
IF 6 SERVINGS IN TOTAL:
0.1 g protein;
trace fat;
0.3 g net carbs;
7 kcal

PER SERVING,
IF 8 SERVINGS IN TOTAL:
0.1 g protein;
trace fat;
0.2 g net carbs;
5 kcal

NUTRITION INFO

IN TOTAL:

1.7 g protein;
0.5 g fat;
6.2 g net carbs;
60 kcal

PER SERVING,
IF 16 SERVINGS IN TOTAL:

0.1 g protein;
trace fat;
0.4 g net carbs;
4 kcal

GUILT-FREE LEMONADE

This easy, four-ingredient crowd-pleaser is relatively mild and sweet, thanks to two different sweeteners: Erythritol and stevia work especially well together, yielding the desired level of sweetness without any bitter aftertaste. Be sure to use freshly squeezed juice from organic lemons for the best taste and healthiest result here. Organic lemons always taste nicest—and, of course, they're free from potentially harmful pesticides.

INGREDIENTS

1 cup (240 ml) freshly squeezed lemon juice

2 quarts (1.9 L) lukewarm water

1 cup (200 g) erythritol crystals

4 teaspoons liquid stevia, or to taste

Lemon slices for garnish (optional)

Yield: 6 servings

Combine all ingredients in a 3-quart (2.8 L) pitcher. Stir until the erythritol is completely dissolved. Refrigerate for a couple of hours until ice cold. Serve over ice cubes or crushed ice and lemon slices.

NUTRITION INFO

IN TOTAL:

trace protein;
trace fat;
trace net carbs;
trace kcal

PER SERVING,
IF 6 SERVINGS IN TOTAL:

trace protein;
trace fat;
trace net carbs;
trace kcal

APPLE PIE—INFUSED WATER

Are you in the mood for sugar-free, calorie-free, all-natural apple pie? I thought so! This is a guilt-free liquid apple pie you can enjoy to your heart's content. It won't spike your blood sugar, as traditional sugar-laden apple pie will, and it's hydrating, too. Be sure to use Ceylon cinnamon here, and in all recipes that call for cinnamon: Unlike the more commonly used cassia, or Chinese cinnamon, it isn't toxic to the liver.

Yield: 6 servings

Place the apple slices, cinnamon sticks, and vanilla bean pieces in a 2-quart (1.9 L) pitcher. Place the grated ginger in a tea ball and close the ball tightly. Place the tea ball in the pitcher and then pour in the water. Refrigerate for at least 5 hours before serving, so that the apple and the vanilla bean have time to release their flavors. Stir gently before serving.

INGREDIENTS

7 ounces (200 g, or about 1 large) sour apple such as Granny Smith, sliced, seeds removed

2 Ceylon cinnamon sticks

1 vanilla bean, cut into 4 pieces (first lengthwise, then crosswise)

1 teaspoon freshly grated ginger

1½ quarts (1.4 L) water

TIP: For a warmer, spicier flavor, omit the vanilla bean and add ½ teaspoon whole cloves to the tea ball together with the grated ginger.

MIGHTY MINT LASSI

In Indian cuisine, lassis are traditional companions for spicy food, and are usually made with yogurt, ice, sweetener, and a variety of spices, such as cumin or turmeric. And both kids and adults love this mild, creamy, cooling, sugar-free version, which is flavored with fresh mint. To make it even more refreshing, add 1 cup (150 g) of crushed ice to the other ingredients and blend well—then sit back and sip.

Yield: 4 servings

Simply place all ingredients in a blender jar and blend until smooth and frothy. Serve over ice cubes—as an accompaniment to spicy food, or on its own as a pick-me-up on a warm day.

INGREDIENTS

2 cups (480 ml) ice-cold water

7 ounces (200 g) plain, organic, full-fat Greek or Turkish yogurt

10 to 15 fresh mint leaves

10 to 15 drops liquid stevia (optional)

NUTRITION INFO

IN TOTAL:
6.5 g protein;
20.0 g fat;
7.4 g net carbs;
239 kcal

PER SERVING,
IF 4 SERVINGS IN TOTAL:
1.6 g protein;
5.0 g;
1.9 g net carbs;
60 kcal

SUPREME ORANGE CREAMSICLE SHAKE

You know those creamy-citrusy ice pops you loved when you were little? Well, I've given them a low-sugar makeover, and now you and your kids can enjoy their great taste in this healthy, dairy-free shake. Add 1 cup (150 g) crushed ice for extra cooling power and an especially slushy result. As it's a drink and a dessert all in one, it's the perfect way to end a light summer meal.

Yield: 1 serving

Simply place all ingredients in a high-speed blender and blend until smooth. Serve immediately.

INGREDIENTS

¼ cup (60 g) **Low-Sugar Orange Marmalade, page 48**

¼ cup (60 ml) **heavy cream or coconut cream**

1 cup (240 ml) **ice-cold unsweetened almond milk**

20 drops **orange stevia**

2 drops **100 percent orange essential oil**

Pinch of **turmeric, for natural orange color (optional)**

TIP: Replace the Low-Sugar Orange Marmalade with Easy Sugar-Free Strawberry Jam (page 51), omit the orange essential oil, and sweeten with vanilla stevia instead of orange stevia, and *voila!*— you've got a low-sugar strawberry shake.

VARIATION: To turn this shake into a power breakfast or snack, add 1 scoop grass-fed, vanilla-flavored whey protein powder before blending.

NUTRITION INFO

IN TOTAL:

3.1 g protein;
23.7 g fat;
5.2 g net carbs;
252 kcal

CREAMY NO-SUGAR HOT CHOCOLATE

Next time you or one of your kids need a mug of something hot, sweet, and comforting, try this nutritious version of traditional hot chocolate. Since it's sugar-free, it won't wreak havoc on your blood sugar, and the dark cocoa powder delivers a healthy hit of minerals, including iron, copper, magnesium, and potassium. It's best served with an ample amount of whipped cream and dark chocolate shavings, but if you don't tolerate dairy, it's easy to make a dairy-free version by using thick coconut cream—preservative-free, if possible—instead.

Yield: 1 serving

Combine all the ingredients in a large mug until well mixed. Top with whipped cream and chocolate shavings, if desired.

INGREDIENTS

¾ cup (180 ml) boiling water

2 tablespoons (28 ml) heavy cream or coconut cream

1 tablespoon (7 g) unsweetened dark cocoa powder

10 drops vanilla stevia, or to taste

NUTRITION INFO

IN TOTAL:
2.0 g protein;
12.0 g fat;
1.5 g net carbs;
122 kcal

HEALTHY PSL (PUMPKIN SPICE LATTE)

Forget those artificially flavored, carb-laden pumpkin spice lattes: They don't contain real pumpkin at all! This healthy version, on the other hand, does. Plus, it not only tastes wonderful, it also nourishes you from head to toe, thanks to the cream and coconut oil, both of which contain healthy fats. Better yet, this easy drink hardly takes more than sixty seconds to make—just mix all ingredients together and enjoy.

Yield: 1 serving

Combine all the ingredients in a large mug and stir until well mixed. (Use an immersion blender for best results, but be careful not to burn yourself when handling hot drinks!) Top with whipped cream, if desired, and serve immediately.

INGREDIENTS

¾ cup (180 ml) boiling water

¼ cup (60 g) 100 percent pure pureed pumpkin

2 tablespoons (28 ml) heavy cream or coconut cream

1 tablespoon (14 g) extra-virgin coconut oil

1 to 2 teaspoons instant espresso powder

½ teaspoon pumpkin pie spice

10 drops vanilla stevia, or to taste

Whipped cream, for garnish (optional)

NUTRITION INFO

IN TOTAL:
1.2 g protein;
25.5 g fat;
4.5 g net carbs;
265 kcal

RICH SUGAR-FREE EGGNOG

Ready for the ultimate eggnog eggsperience? This velvety, mousse-like eggnog is sure to be memorable. Because regular milk contains milk sugar, I use carb-free unsweetened almond milk. Thanks to its rich texture and delicate, lingering taste, you won't miss the milk one bit.

INGREDIENTS

4 eggs, separated*

½ cup (65 g) powdered erythritol

25 drops vanilla stevia, or to taste

1 cup (240 ml) unsweetened almond milk

1 cup plus ½ cup (240 ml plus 120 ml) heavy cream, divided

⅓ cup (80 ml) bourbon whiskey or dark rum (optional)

Freshly grated nutmeg, for serving

*Please note that this recipe contains raw egg white. See the tip for making an egg-free version.

TIP: Don't like your eggnog too thick? Worried about serving raw eggs? Just leave out the beaten egg whites.

NUTRITION INFO

IN TOTAL:
38.9 g protein;
152.9 g fat;
11.8 g net carbs;
1760 kcal

PER SERVING,
IF 8 SERVINGS IN TOTAL:
4.9 g protein;
19.1 g fat;
1.5 g net carbs;
220 kcal

Yield: 8 servings

1. Place the egg yolks, erythritol, vanilla stevia, almond milk, and 1 cup (240 ml) of the heavy cream into a large saucepan. Heat over medium heat, whisking constantly, until the mixture thickens. When it is about to boil, remove it from the heat. Stir in the alcohol, if using. Let cool to room temperature and then refrigerate until cold, about 4 hours.

2. Meanwhile, place the egg whites into a deep, narrow bowl. Beat until soft peaks form. Set aside.

3. Place the remaining ½ cup (120 ml) of cream into a clean bowl. Beat until soft peaks form.

4. Remove the chilled custard from the fridge. Add the beaten egg whites and the whipped heavy cream and whisk until smooth. Refrigerate the eggnog for 1 hour before serving.

5. When you're ready to serve, whisk the eggnog well, pour it into glasses, and grate a little fresh nutmeg on top. Serve immediately.

REFERENCES

Associated Press. "Truvia maker settles Hawaii-based suit for $61 million." December 5, 2014. www.hawaiinewsnow.com/story/27558493/truvia-maker-settles-hawaii-based-suit-for-61m.

Authority Nutrition: An Evidence-Based Approach. https://authoritynutrition.com. Accessed March 9, 2017.

Avena, Nicole M., Pedro Rada, and Bartley G. Hoebel. "Evidence for sugar addiction: Behavioral and neurochemical effects of intermittent, excessive sugar intake." *Neuroscience and Biobehavioral Reviews* 2008 32(1): 20–39.

Birketvedt, GS, M. Shimshi, T. Erling *et al.* "Experiences with three different fiber supplements in weight reduction." *Medical Science Monitor* 2005 Jan; 11(1): 5–8.

Harcombe, Zoë. "Dr. Zoë Harcombe, Ph.D." www.zoeharcombe.com. Accessed March 9, 2017.

Kolp Institute. "Sugar: The Bitter Truth." http://kolpinstitute.org/facts-about-sugar. Accessed March 9, 2017.

Lapis, Trina J, Michael H. Penner, and Juyun Lim. "Humans can taste glucose oligomers independent of the hT1R2/hT1R3 sweet taste receptor." *Chemical Senses* (2016) 41 (9): 755–762

Oklahoma Medical Research Foundation Staff. "New company explores novel therapeutic uses for aspartame." https://omrf.org/2004/08/27/new-company-explores-novel-therapeutic-uses-for-aspartame. 2004.

Rinella, Mary E. "Nonalcoholic fatty liver disease: a systematic review." *JAMA: Journal of the American Medical Association.* 2015;313(22): 2263–2273.

Spreadbury, Ian. "Comparison with ancestral diets suggests dense acellular carbohydrates promote an inflammatory microbiota, and may be the primary dietary cause of leptin resistance and obesity." *Diabetes, Metabolic Syndrome and Obesity: Targets and Therapy.* 2012; 5: 175–189.

Stanhope, Kimber L., Jean Marc Schwarz, Nancy L. Keim, *et al.* "Consuming fructose-sweetened, not glucose-sweetened, beverages increases visceral adiposity and lipids and decreases insulin sensitivity in overweight/obese humans." *The Journal of Clinical Investigation* 2009 119(5): 1322–1334.

U. S. Department of Agriculture. "Sugar and Sweeteners Yearbook Table." www.ers.usda.gov/data-products/sugar-and-sweeteners-yearbook-tables.aspx. Accessed March 9, 2017.

WebMD. "The Truth on Artificial Sweeteners." www.webmd.com/food-recipes/features/truth-artificial-sweeteners#1. 2002.

Yang, Quanhe, Zefeng Zhang, and Edward W Gregg. "Added Sugar Intake and Cardiovascular Diseases Mortality Among US Adults." *JAMA Internal Medicine* 2014 174(4): 516–524.

RESOURCES

Books

Bowden, Jonny and Sinatra, Stephen. 2012. *The Great Cholesterol Myth: Why Lowering Your Cholesterol Won't Prevent Heart Disease—and the Statin-Free Plan That Will*. Beverly, MA: Fair Winds Press.

Braly, James and Hoggan, Ron. 2002. *Dangerous Grains: Why Gluten Cereal Grains May Be Hazardous To Your Health*. New York: Avery Books.

Davis, William. 2011. *Wheat Belly: Lose the Wheat, Lose the Weight, and Find Your Path Back to Health*. New York: Rodale, Inc.

Eenfeldt, Andreas. 2014. *Low Carb, High Fat Food Revolution: Advice and Recipes to Improve Your Health and Reduce Your Weight*. New York: Skyhorse Publishing.

Evans, David. 2012. *Cholesterol and Saturated Fat Prevent Heart Disease: Evidence from 101 Scientific Papers*. Surrey: Grosvenor House Publishing Ltd.

Feinman, Richard. 2014. *The World Turned Upside Down: The Second Low-Carbohydrate Revolution*. USA: NMS Press-Duck-in-a-Boat LLC.

Gedgaudas, Nora. 2011. *Primal Body, Primal Mind: Beyond the Paleo Diet for Total Health and a Longer Life*. Rochester, VT: Healing Arts Press.

Kendrick, Malcolm. 2008. *The Great Cholesterol Con: The Truth about What Really Causes Heart Disease and How to Avoid It*. London: John Blake Publishing.

Kendrick, Malcolm. 2015. *Doctoring Data: How to Sort Out Medical Advice from Medical Nonsense*. Cwmbran, Wales: Columbus Publishing Ltd.

Lustig, Robert. 2012. *Fat Chance: Beating the Odds against Sugar, Processed Food, Obesity, and Disease*. New York Hudson Street Press.

Minger, Denise. 2013. *Death by Food Pyramid: How Shoddy Science, Sketchy Politics and Shady Special Interests Have Ruined Our Health*. Oxford, CA: Primal Blueprint Publishing.

Moore, Jimmy and Westman, Eric C. 2013. *Cholesterol Clarity: What the HDL Is Wrong with My Numbers?* Las Vegas, NV: Victory Belt Publishing.

Noakes, Tim, *et al.* 2015. *The Real Meal Revolution: The Radical, Sustainable Approach to Healthy Eating (Age of Legends)*. London: Constable & Robinson Ltd.

Perlmutter, David. 2013. *Grain Brain: The Surprising Truth about Wheat, Carbs, and Sugar—Your Brain's Silent Killers*. New York: Little, Brown and Company.

Taubes, Gary. 2008. *Good Calories, Bad Calories: Fats, Carbs, and the Controversial Science of Diet and Health*. New York: Anchor Books.

_____. 2010. *Why We Get Fat: And What to Do About It*. New York: Alfred A. Knopf.

_____. 2016. *The Case Against Sugar*. New York: Alfred A. Knopf.

Teicholz, Nina. 2014. *The Big Fat Surprise: Why Butter, Meat and Cheese Belong in a Healthy Diet*. New York: Simon & Schuster, Inc.

Yudkin, John. 2013 (1972). *Pure, White and Deadly: How Sugar Is Killing Us and What We Can Do to Stop It*. New York: Penguin Books.

Blogs

www.lowcarbsosimple.com
www.alldayidreamaboutfood.com
www.ketodietapp.com/blog
www.mariamindbodyhealth.com
www.peaceloveandlowcarb.com
www.sugarfreemom.com
www.lowcarbmaven.com
www.lowcarbyum.com
www.ditchthecarbs.com

ABOUT THE AUTHOR

Elviira Krebber, a Finnish blogger and photographer, is the creator of the popular *Low-Carb, So Simple* blog, which features easy and innovative sugar-free recipes with five ingredients or less that are suitable for a gluten-free, clean eating lifestyle. More than a decade ago, she healed herself with a gluten-free, low-sugar diet, and has been an avid promoter of a starch-free, low-sugar lifestyle ever since. She is currently studying to be a nutrition therapist. She is also the author of several eBooks and a printed book in Finnish, called *Healing Ketosis— Get Healthy with Gluten-Free, Sugar-Free Food*. She speaks about ketogenic and low-sugar lifestyle both nationally and internationally.

ACKNOWLEDGMENTS

I would like to thank my parents for always supporting and trusting me even if you didn't always agree with what I was doing. A special thanks to my husband; my blog and this book would never exist without your love and support.

INDEX